Ingenious Shop Aids & Jigs

Ingenious Shop Aids & Jigs

Professional Shortcuts for the Home Workshop

Graham McCulloch

 Sterling Publishing Co., Inc. New York

Library of Congress Cataloging-in-Publication Data

McCulloch, Graham.
 Ingenious shop aids & jigs : professional shortcuts for the home
workshop / by Graham McCulloch.
     p.   cm.
 Includes index.
 ISBN 0-8069-0300-7
 1. Woodwork—Amateurs' manuals. 2. Woodworking tools—Amateurs'
manuals. 3. Workshops—Equipment and supplies—Amateurs' manuals.
I. Title. II. Title: Ingenious shop aids and jigs.
TT185.M214 1993
684′.08—dc20   92-45041
                                                         CIP

10 9 8 7 6 5 4 3 2 1

Published by Sterling Publishing Company, Inc.
387 Park Avenue South, New York, N.Y. 10016
© 1993 by Graham McCulloch
Distributed in Canada by Sterling Publishing
℅ Canadian Manda Group, P.O. Box 920, Station U
Toronto, Ontario, Canada M8Z 5P9
Distributed in Great Britain and Europe by Cassell PLC
Villiers House, 41/47 Strand,
London WC2N 5JE, England
Distributed in Australia by Capricorn Link Ltd.
P.O. Box 665, Lane Cove, NSW 2066
Manufactured in the United States of America

Sterling ISBN 0-8069-0300-7

Dedication

To Gwen,
for your unending support.

Contents

APPENDICES 207

Introduction

Ever since my introduction as a young boy into wood-working, I have had a strong desire to have a home work-shop. After designing trade-show exhibits and having them built by outside contractors, I decided that the most expedient way to build a workshop was to do it myself. This solved the problem of having to go to the contractor's shop on a regular basis to verify dimensions, work quality, and materials. And, of course, to envy them.

As a result of my desire to build trade-show exhibits, I opened my own shop. It was a modest operation then and still is today, at least by commercial woodworking shop standards. It doesn't have all the sophisticated equipment that commercial shops have, but the equipment that I do have works well for me. One of the main reasons is because of the techniques that I use in the shop. I learned some of these shortcuts during my "manual training" sessions in public school. I discovered many more through my experience as a commercial interior designer, design-ing and supervising the construction of offices, stores, and other commercial ventures. Of particular help was the opportunity to watch the "old hands" who actually did the woodwork on the job sites.

This book is not about how to build a particular book-case, birdfeeder, or china cabinet. There are no wood-working plans in it. It is, however, a book that will help you save time and improve the accuracy in building these projects. Photographs will illustrate how to accomplish these shortcuts. This book is not designed for the novice do-it-yourselfer, but is aimed at the more knowledgeable woodworker.

Ingenious Shop Aids & Jigs is written in an encyclope-dia style to make it easier to find the shortcuts that refer to the particular tool or technique that you may be using at the time. These tools and techniques appear in alphabeti-

Author Graham McCulloch is his workshop.

cal order. Cross-references are made to simplify the some-times confusing terminology used to describe some tools and equipment. For example, if you look up sandpaper, reference would be made to abrasives, a more all-encompassing term.

A few words of advice before you move on: First, I would suggest that you look over the information con-tained in the book before making full use of it on your workbench. Second, in the following pages you will come across many jigs that can be made in the shop. Exact dimensions for these jigs are not given because they may not be suited for your specific needs. Finally, before you delve into the book read the chapter on safety, even if you are not a novice in woodworking.

Graham McCulloch

CHAPTER 1
Safety Instructions

Safety in the workshop should be of utmost concern to each and every woodworker. Pay attention to the following guidelines:

1. Read, understand, and obey *all* safety instructions that come with the tools that you have. They are given to ensure your safety.

2. Wear the proper safety equipment (Illus. 1-1). This includes safety glasses and hearing protection. Sawdust poses a health problem, so use an efficient dust collector or exhaust fan, and wear a filter mask. Some types of wood give off highly **toxic** dust when they are cut or sanded.

3. Use all the safety equipment that is on your tools. This includes the guards.

4. Keep your mind on your work and avoid distractions. If you're angry about something, go for a walk. Stay out of your workshop.

5. Don't drink or use drugs in your workshop. If you are taking any drugs or medication, stay away from your tools.

Woodworking is a satisfying, enjoyable hobby. Have fun. Enjoy and make use of this book. Work safely.

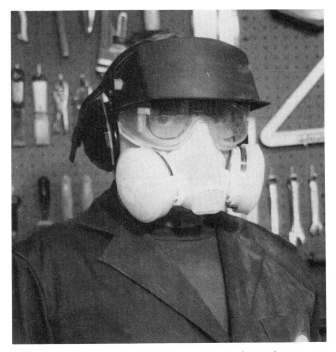

Illus. 1-1. Make sure that you wear safety glasses, hearing protection, and a dust filter when working in your workshop.

CHAPTER 2
The Workshop

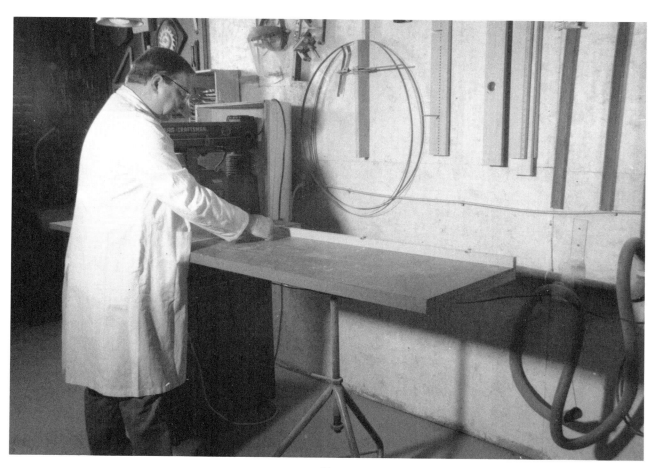

Planning a Workshop

Without question, the best workshop layout is the one that works best for you. The information in this chapter contains reliable time-tested guidelines for initially setting up a workshop. There are two determinations that have to be made when designing a workshop: how to lay out your power tools and where to place these tools in relation to each other. A U-shaped configuration is the best layout for your stationary power tools.

If you take any woodworking project through its natural steps, a logical layout will evolve. For example, you start with the rough lumber. Therefore, a thickness planer would be the first power tool used. Cutting would be next, followed maybe by shaping, drilling, or planing/joining, with sanding being the final step before finishing. You will have to determine how much space is required for each of these tools. This varies from machine to machine. For instance, a table saw takes up more space than a radial arm saw, because with a table saw you have to walk around the tool on all four sides.

One technique that will prove helpful is to set up all your stationary power-tool work surfaces at the same height as your table or radial arm saw. This will reduce the overall required space. If your workbench is also at the same height, it can also be used as an out-feed or in-feed table for your saw or thickness planer. Following are techniques for a basic workshop that will help you save space and create a very comfortable and efficient work environment.

The Basic Workshop

The basic workshop shown in Illus. 2-1 is an area 10 × 20 feet that will fit in most basements. Planning should include a provision to bring in 4 × 8-foot sheets of plywood and to remove large, finished projects. In this workshop,

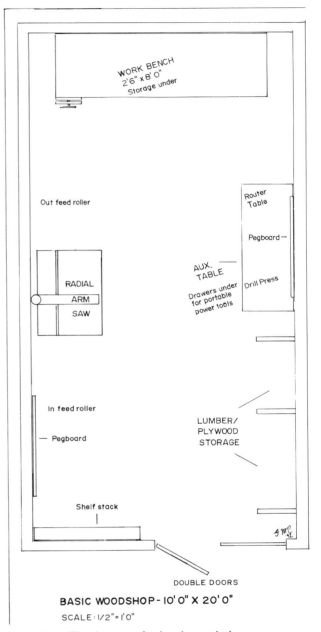

Illus. 2-1. The layout of a basic workshop.

the radial arm saw is used as the basic tool because of its versatility. The other major power tools are bench-mounted. Portable power tools are stored in drawers under the worktable. It includes two pegboards, but you can include as many as are necessary. Mount them close to the stationary tools to hold their accessories.

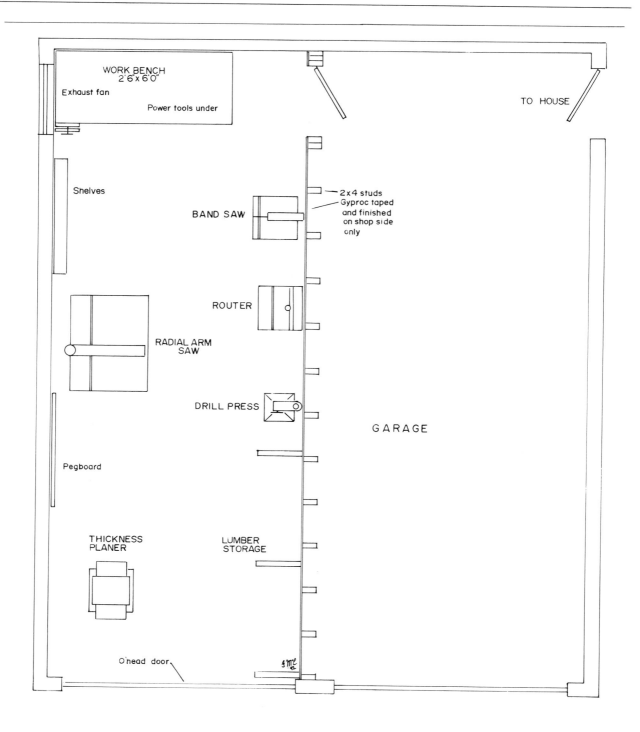

DOUBLE GARAGE WOODSHOP

SCALE: 1/2" = 1'0"

Illus. 2-2. The layout for a workshop in a two-car garage.

If you have a central built-in vacuum, purchase an additional length of hose to use in your shop and either have your dealer install an additional outlet within the shop area or do it yourself.

Ventilation is something you should provide for. It is essential that a good fan is installed in a window or through a wall to the outside.

Gypsum (plasterboard) on 2×4-inch studs is a good material to use for the walls, but make sure that they have tight seams and fit tightly to the floor and ceiling. Two-by-four-foot plain acoustical tiles will suffice for the ceiling. A concrete floor is ideal. If not, a solid raised floor will do. Before moving any of the tools in, give the shop two or three good coats of a quality paint. This will likely be the first and last time that the shop is painted.

Finally, this basic workshop has lots of room for expansion if you plan it right. Leave room outside the shop area to relocate the lumber storage and the auxiliary worktable; this will provide space in the shop for new stationary power tools.

The Double-Car Garage Workshop

If you are willing to leave your car outside or have only one car and are fortunate to have a two-car garage, you can create a great workshop for very little money and with very little work (Illus. 2-2).

The advantage of this type of workshop is the overhead door access. In the summertime or in warmer climates, you can leave the door open while working. This will minimize the dust problem and make it easier to bring in materials and remove finished projects. However, make sure there is *always* some adult in the shop when the door is open. Kids love tools.

To build this workshop, do the following: add a gypsum (plasterboard) divider wall on 2×4-inch studs and an interior door; paint (several good coats) the floor and walls; add an outlet in the shop area if your house has a built-in central vacuum, and install more lights, electrical outlets, and a **good** exhaust fan. The workshop is ready to be used. For later expansion, your lumber storage could be put in the garage area or you might build a lean-to attached to the outside wall.

The L-Shaped Workshop

The L-shaped workshop is my favorite type of shop. The only power tool unaccounted for in the plans for the shop shown in Illus. 2-3 is a stroke sander. This layout maximizes the use of space while making room for just about all the stationary power tools that are needed. Without utilizing the expansion area, the assembly of larger projects and the crosscutting of plywood sheets can be done in the area between the table saw and the jointer.

Although in Illus. 2-3 there is only one pegboard, which is located over the worktable, the ideal workshop will have one hanging by every stationary tool. It is also recommended that the thickness planer and the jointer be mounted on locking casters so that they may be easily moved to provide even more assembly room. Portable tool storage would be under the worktable. As well as ambient lighting, be sure to provide individual lighting over each of the stationary tools.

Templates

You can cut out or photocopy the templates shown in Illus. 2-4 to assist you in setting up a workshop. They represent the most commonly used stationary power tools and are drawn close to scale. The scale used here is $1'' = 1'0''$.

Floors and Ceilings

Any type of flooring will suffice, as long as it is solid and will support a lot of weight. I've found, however, that a

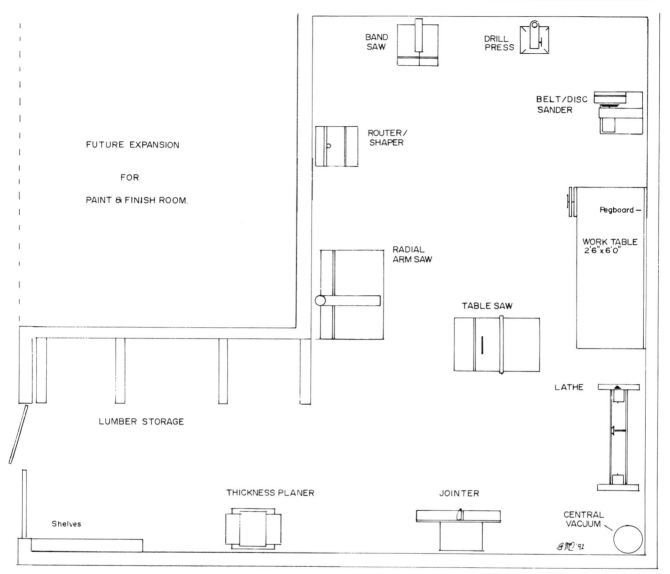

Illus. 2-3. The layout for an L-shaped workshop.

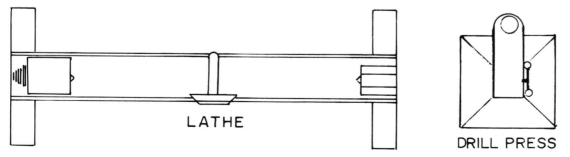

Illus. 2-4. These templates and those on the following page represent the commonly used stationary power tools. Use them to determine a layout for your workshop.

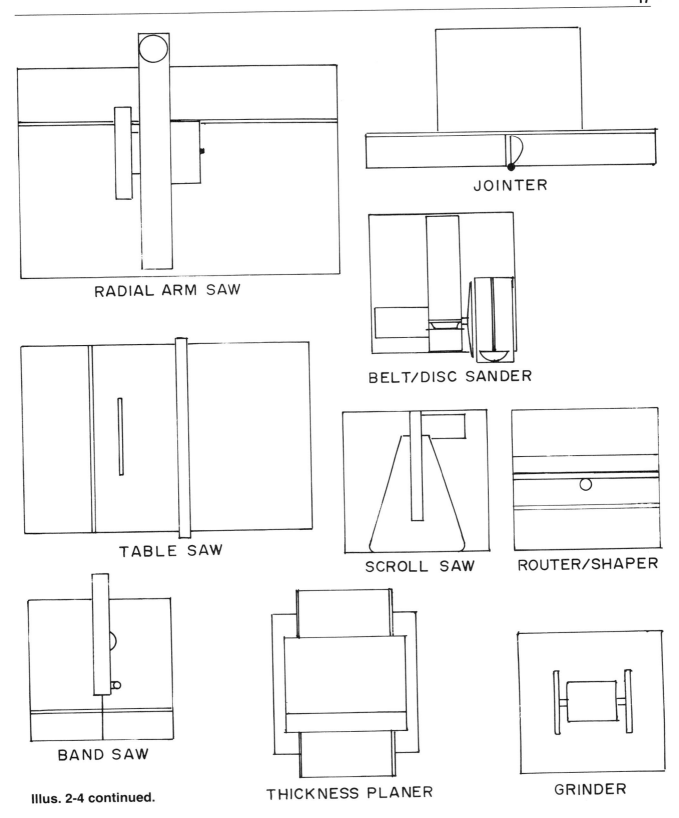

RADIAL ARM SAW

JOINTER

BELT/DISC SANDER

TABLE SAW

SCROLL SAW

ROUTER/SHAPER

BAND SAW

THICKNESS PLANER

GRINDER

Illus. 2-4 continued.

concrete floor is best. Before moving your equipment in, give the floor three or four coats of a good epoxy floor paint. Epoxy paint may be more expensive, but it will outlast most other types and this will probably be the only time that you will have to paint your floor. I painted my floor in 1988. I work in my shop daily and the floor still looks new.

Consider insulating your workshop, not necessarily against the heat or the cold, but against the noise and the dust. Fibreglass batts between the ceiling joists and the wall studs will greatly decrease the noise and dust level in adjoining areas. Inexpensive wallboard or gypsum board is all that is necessary to cover the walls and ceiling with, but do make sure you install a polyethylene barrier first. If there are exposed heating ducts, wrap them with fibreglass and polyethylene as these are excellent sound transmitters. Make sure that the inside doors have weatherstripping all around them to further confine the dust. Some people actually ''wrap'' the room in polyethylene after insulating and before installing the gypsum board.

Lighting

Good lighting is essential. A couple of 2 × 4-foot fluorescent fixtures on the ceiling should be adequate as a general lighting arrangement for most home workshops, but you should also add more (Illus. 2-5).

Direct lighting is also required (Illus. 2-6). There is nothing worse than trying to cut on a line that you can barely see because the tool you are using is casting a shadow over it. Try to have direct lighting over each stationary power tool. The ones that really require it are the drill press, band saw and radial arm saw, because the housings of these tools are located over the tables and will cause annoying shadows. Suspended incandescent lamps or gooseneck lamps are the best source of light for these tools.

Your workbench should also be well lit. This can be accomplished by installing a suspended fluorescent fixture over it or by hanging a lamp from a drapery track so that it can be focused over the work at hand. Individual light switches are fine, but it is better if you have a power box with circuit breakers either in or right next to your workshop. This will eliminate the need for separate switches.

If you are doing a lot of work with veneers, fluorescent

Illus. 2-5. Task lighting is required on tools such as this.

Illus. 2-6. Direct lighting is also required when working in a workshop.

lighting is needed when you are selecting the flitches. Fluorescent lighting is also helpful when you are choosing paint colors.

Many of the larger power tools can be used on either 110 or 220 voltage. This being the case, it is more economical in the long haul to hook them up to a 220-volt outlet.

Electrical System

Nothing is more frustrating than turning on the saw at the same time that your husband or wife has just turned on the vacuum cleaner in the next room, and the circuit breaker "pops." To prevent this, get a qualified electrician to examine the area that you are going to use as a workshop once you have preliminary plans for its layout. Show or describe to the electrician the tools you have or are planning to obtain, so that adequate power can be supplied. Most stationary power tools require a dedicated circuit because of the amount of power that they draw (Illus. 2-7).

Illus. 2-7. It is better if you have a power box with circuit breakers in or near your workshop.

Ventilation

An effective ventilation system is extremely important in a workshop. Not only is the dust from some types of wood highly toxic, but a dust buildup is highly volatile as well. Ideally, a workshop should be fitted with a built-in dust collector, with ductwork and stop gates at every machine that will keep the dust to a minimum. Failing this, a good, heavy-duty shop vacuum will suffice (Illus. 2-8). Connect it to the exhaust ports that are found on most stationary and portable tools. Another method is to buy a built-in vacuum for your house and have the installer run extra plastic pipe and outlets into your workshop.

Illus. 2-8. The workshop should be supplied with some type of dust-collection system.

I don't have a built-in unit, but I ran some vacuum pipe into my shop and had it connected to a modified wet/dry shop vacuum in another room. I made plugs to insert in the openings that are not being used. The vacuum tank is a used plastic drum that I found. I used a utility knife to cut off the top and then modified the top to take a used commercial vacuum head that I purchased very cheaply from a janitorial service company. The flexible hoses were bought from the same company.

In addition to a vacuum, a good exhaust fan installed in a window in your workshop will certainly lessen the dust accumulation in your shop and in your home. Although some sawdust is toxic when inhaled, it is generally not harmful in such small quantities.

Dust collectors will not remove all the dust, nor will they remove toxic fumes like the odors from contact cement and plastic wood, etc. An adequate ventilating fan is also a necessity (Illus. 2-9). This will be proven out the first time that you do wood finishing and find the surface rough with dust after the finish has dried.

Illus. 2-9. An adequate ventilating fan is also needed in the workshop.

Lumber Storage

Lumber (softwood and plywood) and hardwood should be stored in a dry area and off the floor, especially if the floor is untreated concrete. Ideally, plywood should be stored flat, unless you are going to use it within the next couple of days. It can also be stored in a vertical position if it is braced so that it is truly vertical. Lumber and hardwood should be laid out flat and off the floor with supports every two feet or so. Laths or slats should be placed between the layers in the same position as the supports. This allows air to circulate around the wood so it can "breathe" and air-dry.

Depending on the geographical area in which you live, you should occasionally check for bugs or insects that may have arrived with your new lumber. If you see any, exterminate them. If not, they may start drilling holes in your lumber and, if hungry enough, may start working on your house.

Don't go to the lumber yard today to buy wood for a project that you want to start tomorrow. Wood has to acclimatize. If you insist on doing the job tomorrow, you will probably have to buy kiln-dried lumber at a substantially higher price. An alternate approach—one that will save you money—is to buy air-dried wood and plan on starting the hutch next month.

Green wood will shrink by at least ¼ inch in width and length. Its thickness will decrease as well when it is brought indoors to dry. The dimensions of kiln-dried woods may change when they are brought into the workshop. This is because your shop area may be more humid than your lumber dealer's, so, therefore, your wood may absorb moisture, increasing its dimensions.

Consideration should be given to the storage location so that stock can be easily moved from the workshop into the storage area and from the storage area into the workshop. Make sure also that the door to the outside and the doors to your shop are wide enough to handle both the lumber and the various projects that you make.

Tool Storage

Throughout this book, you will find a number of ways to

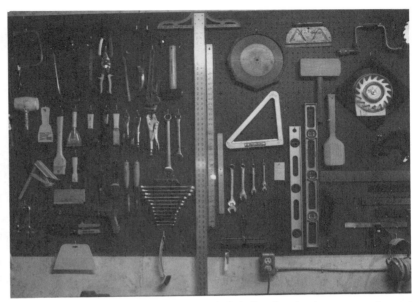

Illus. 2-10 (above left). A drawer method of storing tools. **Illus. 2-11 (above right).** Storing tools on a pegboard.

store your hand tools and portable power tools (Illus. 2-10 and 2-11). These range from pegboards to storage cabinets, most of which hang on the wall. So, before moving all your stationary power tools into position, determine where you want to hang the storage units, and put up the required brackets or supports. By doing this beforehand, you won't have to climb over your stationary tools.

Telephone

One device that will prove extremely helpful in the workshop is a phone flasher that can be bought at an electronics shop (Illus. 2-12). The phone flasher is a strobe light that flashes when the phone rings, and will really grab your attention.

Visitors in the Workshop

Many woodworkers like to have visitors in their workshop

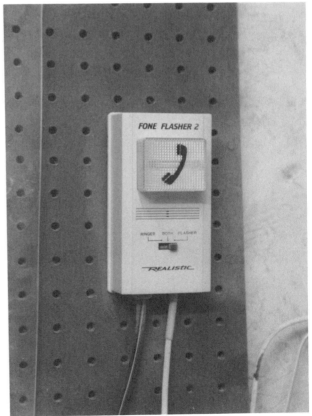

Illus. 2-12. A phone flasher will prove to be very helpful in the workshop.

while they are working. They get to show off their woodworking skills.

Be forewarned, however. Accidents can and usually do happen when you least expect them. Make sure your guest(s) are wearing the proper safety gear if you continue working on a project while they are there. Also, it is advisable to have a Do Not Enter sign on the door to your workshop (Illus. 2-13). This will prevent visitors from sneaking into the workshop and surprising you while you are working.

Securing Power Tools

The best way to keep your portable power tools safe and away from children or the inexperienced is to lock up your workshop or keep your tools locked in a cabinet. Sometimes, though, this isn't convenient.

If you have to leave your tools out, or your shop unlocked, buy inexpensive, small padlocks like the one shown in Illus. 2-14. Insert the hasp through the plug prong holes and lock them. You may be able to lock up three of four tools with one padlock. If the prong holes are too small, drill them to size.

Illus. 2-13 (above left). It is advisable to put a Do Not Enter sign on the door leading to your workshop, to prevent visitors from entering unexpectedly. **Illus. 2-14 (above right).** Small padlocks can be used to lock up power tools.

C H A P T E R   3
Shop Aids, Jigs and Other Shortcuts

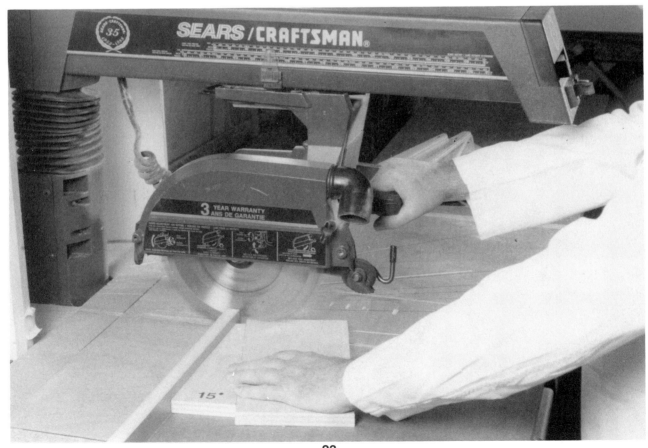

Abrasives

(Also see Belt Sander, Drum Sander, Random Sanders, Orbital Sander, Sander Belts, and Steel Wool)

Types of Abrasive

Abrasives come in all shapes and forms. There are the powders such as pumice, emery, and rottenstone. There are the conventional sanding papers that come in ¼, ½, and full sheets and discs. These can be paper-, adhesive-, or cloth-backed. Sanding paper with a Velcro®-type backing has recently become available. To add to the variety, there are belts and drums that are available in myriad sizes and descriptions.

Steel wool is considered an abrasive and is generally available in seven different grades. More recently, there has been the introduction of abrasives with trade names such as Bear-Tex®, by Norton Co. These are synthetic abrasives that are reminiscent of the plastic pot scrubbers that have been around for a while. Bear-Tex and its competitors are available in a variety of grades and types.

Commonly found now in hardware stores are Flex'n Sand® sanding blocks. These are foam pads that usually have a different grit on each of the large faces, i.e., fine/medium, medium/coarse.

Illus. 3-1 shows some of the materials currently on the market.

Sandpaper

Descriptions

Modern, coated abrasives (sandpaper) have a flexible or semi-rigid backing to which abrasive grains are bonded by an adhesive. The usual backings used in the manufacture of sandpaper are cloth, paper, vulcanized fibre, polyester film, or a combination. The most common abrasives being used today are zirconia alumina, ceramic aluminum oxide, aluminum oxide, silicon carbide, garnet, emery, crocus, diamond, and chrome oxide.

Grain (Grit) Coverage

Coated abrasives are generally made in two levels of abrasive grain surface density: close coat and open coat. A close-coat product is one in which the grains completely cover the surface of the backing. The greater number of abrading points per square inch normally results in a larger amount of material being removed before the product becomes worn and unusable.

An open-coat product is one in which the abrasive grains cover about 50 to 60 percent of the backing. Open-coat products offer greater flexibility, but may not provide as good a finish as close-coat products. Open-coat sandpaper frequently cuts faster and provides greater resistance to "loading." Wood finish coats, soft metals, and fibreglass are typical applications for open-coat products.

Sandpaper Sheets and Discs The biggest problem that the home woodworker has when purchasing sandpaper by the sheet is determining which type of sheet to buy. First, do not buy sandpaper that does not have a grade

Illus. 3-1. Some commonly available abrasives.

Grit Number	Description	0/0 Number	
50	very coarse	1	
60	very coarse	1/2–0	
80	coarse	1/0	
100	very coarse	2/0	
120	medium	3/0	**Chart. 3-1.**
150	medium	4/0	
180	medium	5/0	
220	fine	6/0	
240	fine	7/0	
280	fine	8/0	
320	very fine	9/0	
400	very fine	10/0	

number, e.g., 120, 240, etc. There does not seem to be an industry standard as to what grits are being used when the paper is labelled "Fine," "Medium," "Coarse." A "medium" sheet of sandpaper can have grits ranging from 36–1,200. Quality products have the company's brand name on them, a grit number, a label (i.e., medium), and a brief description of the product and what the product is recommended for.

For woodworking and treated (primed, sealed, lacquered or painted) surfaces two good types of sandpaper to use are open-coat garnet and open-coat silicon carbide. The *best* types to use are open-coat aluminum oxide and open-coat zirconia alumina.

The weight of the paper backing also is a factor when selecting sandpaper. Both have to be durable. For example, thin backing would not last long in a high-speed palm sander.

Every abrasive manufacturer has a different name or code to identify its vast array of backings. The best way to determine if sandpaper has a suitable back is through trial and error. If you find that the paper tears or breaks down prematurely, make note not to buy it again. Also, be aware that sandpaper that is slightly more expensive, such as Norton® or 3M® sandpaper, will generally last considerably longer than less expensive sandpaper if it is used in the correct application.

Purchasing Sandpaper Belts and Drums   The *best* type of sandpaper to use in belt or drum form is open-coat zirconia alumina. Open-coat aluminum oxide is also *good* to use. The same rules for purchasing sheets of sandpaper apply to purchasing sandpaper in belt and drum form.

Grades of Sandpaper

Sandpaper may be graded in one or all of three ways. This grading system can confuse the home workshopper. The information provided in this section will help clarify this system.

The grading of a sheet of sandpaper is found on its back and has either one of two numbering systems or a word description. Chart 3-1 presents a sampling of these systems.

The grits increase in numbers up to 1,200. Sandpaper that is 1,200 grit is considered ultra-fine. The grits also decrease down. Thirty-six-grit sandpaper is industrial-grade sandpaper.

The 0/0 numbers are called "oughts." This is an old system of rating sandpaper. For example, a fine grade of sandpaper is called eight-ought paper.

Types of Sandpaper

In addition to the various grit numbers on sandpaper, there are a number of different sandpaper types, as previously

Grit Type	General Application	
Flint paper	Softwoods	
Garnet paper	Soft to medium hardwoods	
Aluminum oxide	Softwoods and hardwoods	
Emery paper (wet or dry)	Between finish coats or on soft metals such as aluminum	**Chart. 3-2.**
Emery cloth (wet or dry)	Between finish coats or on soft metals, but mostly on soft metals.	

Illus. 3-2. Sandpaper is available in different grades.

mentioned. A general rule of thumb for the various grit types and their common applications is shown in Chart 3-2.

Using Sandpaper

You should rarely use very coarse or coarse sandpaper in your workshop. These types of sandpaper cut too deeply into the woods, and the cuts are extremely difficult to remove. If your tools are kept sharp, your first sanding should be with a medium (120–180) grit sandpaper.

If you are using an orbital sander, always run the sander in the direction of the grain and use nothing lower than a 120-grit sandpaper.

A high-speed orbital or palm finishing sander should not be used with anything lower than a 180-grit sandpaper,

as it will slow the machine down and work it too hard, resulting in a possible motor burnout. Generally, if you have "swirls" on your stock after sanding, you have probably applied too much pressure on the sander.

Jigs for Cutting Sandpaper

With these jigs you will save a lot of time cutting sandpaper. To make these jigs, cut a piece of hardwood or plywood to the exact size of your orbital sander pad (Illus. 3-3). Mitre the long side. Drill a hole at the top center for pegboard hanging, and you now have a jig for cutting your sandpaper to fit your sander.

A similar jig can be made for a ¼-sheet palm sander, but the mitre must be cut on two edges (Illus. 3-5).

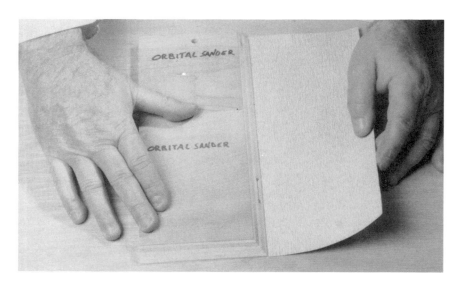

Illus. 3-3. Make a jig the exact size of your orbital sander pad.

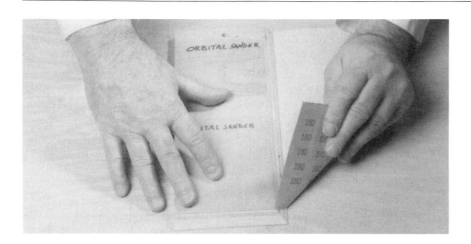

Illus. 3-4. Mitre the long side of the wood.

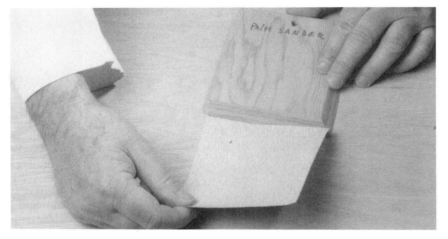

Illus. 3-5. Jig for a palm sander.

Sandpaper Storage

Sandpaper sheets have a tendency to curl when left on a shelf or in a drawer. To properly store sandpaper, you should leave it in its original cardboard package. If the sandpaper comes in a wrapping of paper or plastic, as so many products do these days, remove it because humidity will build up and cause curling. The best way to store all sandpaper, though, is to lay it flat, abrasive side down, on a shelf or in a drawer with a weight on it (Illus. 3-6). Sanding belts or drums should be stored either on edge or hanging from a dowel.

Illus. 3-6. The best way to store all sandpaper is to lay it flat on a shelf or in a drawer with a weight on it.

Used Sandpaper

Instead of throwing away sheets of sandpaper that I have just removed from my sanders, I store them and use them for hand-sanding jobs (Illus. 3-7). After being used on the sanders, they become much more pliable and are easier to use for hand-sanding than a fresh sheet.

Sanding Discs

A quick-change sanding disc has been invented (Illus. 3-8). This product—sold by different manufacturers—

doesn't leave a residue on the backing plate as the adhesive ones do.

This new product has a fabric on it, and its backing plate has hooks on it. It is also available with adapters for palm and orbital sanders. Though the product is relatively expensive, it will save a great deal of time, aggravation, and waste.

Steel Wool

Chart 3-3 contains grading and general-application information for steel wool.

Illus. 3-7. Store old sandpaper to use for hand-sanding jobs.

Illus. 3-8. This new, commercially available sanding disc is available with adapters for palm and orbital sanders.

GRADE	USAGE
No. 3	coarse, for rust removal after soaking in a light oil
No. 2	medium-coarse, for wax removal on floors
No. 1	medium-coarse, for cleaning copper pipe ends for soldering
No. 0	fine, for coarse sanding or paint removal
No. 00	very fine, for cleaning brass, copper, and suede
No. 000	extra-fine, for final wood sanding
No. 0000	super-fine, for sanding between finishing coats, and for putting a satin sheen on metals and plastic
NOTE:	*Never* use steel wool on wood if the finish that you are going to use is *water*-based.

Chart 3-3.

Illus. 3-9. Steel wool is available in different grades.

Pumice Powder

I always keep a small amount of pumice powder on hand (Illus. 3-10). This is an inexpensive product that is available from most hardware stores.

Pumice powder is used as a final rubdown for fine furniture finishes. After a final coat of satin polyurethane, I pour some boiled linseed oil on the surface, sprinkle on some pumice powder and, using a soft cloth, rub the finish with the grain to put a glassy, smooth final finish on the project. After doing this, pour a little paint thinner onto the surface and wipe off any remaining pumice and oil residue.

Adhesives

(Also see Tape, Epoxy Glue, Glue, and Rubber Cement)

Types of Adhesive

Following is a description of some of the commonly available types of adhesive (Illus. 3-11).

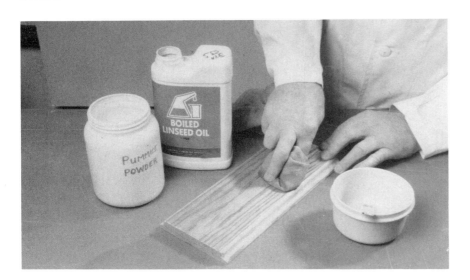

Illus. 3-10. Always have a small amount of pumice powder available. It will prove very helpful in the workshop.

Illus. 3-11. Some of the commonly available adhesives.

Acrylic solvent is a clear liquid that is used for bonding Plexiglas® to other plastics such as polystyrene and acrylics. It is applied sparingly and carefully because it will readily run. It is generally applied with a hypodermic needle. This unites the molecules of the two pieces and creates a very strong joint. Curing takes about an hour.

Contact cement adheres itself instantaneously upon contact. It is available in a regular form or as a water-based product. Water-based contact cement is used on plastics. Regular contact cement is used for applying wood veneer, wood joints, and plastic laminates. You apply the contact cement to both surfaces, let it semi-dry, clamp the surfaces together, and let them dry overnight.

Epoxy resin comes in two parts that have to be mixed in equal amounts. It has excellent strength qualities. It will fill gaps and is waterproof. Though it is not usually considered a woodworking glue, it will make strong repairs to such things as chair and table legs.

Hot glue is sold in sticks for use in a hot-melt glue gun. There are different types of glue sticks available, so read the container labels carefully. If the label does not describe a specific use, it is probably a general-purpose glue. There is even a caulking stick available for small jobs. This is a good repair adhesive that sets up quickly and is excellent for tacking things together.

Rubber cement is excellent for paper materials and for tacking materials together for making duplicate patterns such as on a band saw. For permanent paper or cardboard adhesions, apply the rubber cement to both surfaces, let it semi-dry, and then press the surfaces together. For tacking wood together, apply rubber cement in small spots to one

Illus. 3-12. Spray-on adhesive.

side and then hold the two pieces together for a few minutes.

Urea resin comes in a powder form and has to be mixed with water to a syrupy consistency. It does not stain the wood and is not affected by solvents or thinners. The pieces being joined must be fitted together tightly.

White glue is a general-purpose woodworkers' glue that sets up fairly quickly, but requires clamping. Clean up the seepage with water immediately.

Carpenter's glue is a synthetic resin adhesive that is designed for high-quality woodworking. It has a good initial tack, is quick-setting, and has a high shear strength. Assembly time is 15–20 minutes, and clamping time is one hour.

Marine glue is a plastic resin powder adhesive with a chemical hardener to improve water resistance. As its name implies, it is used for boats. It is also used for any exterior projects such as outdoor furniture. This product is mixed with water to a syrup consistency. Mix only that amount which you will use in a couple of hours. It has a clamping time of six hours.

Spray-on Adhesives

Many manufacturers produce a spray-on adhesive product that should be kept around the workshop (3-12). These adhesives help keep sanding discs on, or you can use the adhesive to make your own sanding discs. Spray-on adhesives can also be used to tack paper patterns to workpieces.

Angles

(Also see Mitres, under type of tool used, and Rafter Angles)

Finding the Centers of Angles

Here is a technique for finding the centers of angles (Illus. 3-13–3-15). When cutting out triangles, hexagonals, octagonals, etc., don't throw away the off-cuts.

For example, if you want to drill a hole in the middle of a triangular piece of wood, use double-face or masking tape to reattach an off-cut to one or more sides of the triangle, so that when you are using a square, one side will be "true." Now, draw a line vertically across the piece. Move the off-cut to another side of the triangular piece and

Illus. 3-13. The off-cuts and the triangle.

Illus. 3-14. The off-cuts reattached to the triangle with double-faced tape. Note the Plexiglas® that fills in the saw kerf.

Illus. 3-15. The center point for the lines.

repeat the process. Now repeat this process one more time and you will end up with converging lines. Where they converge is the center point, as shown in Illus. 3-14.

I use a piece of ⅛-inch Plexiglas to fill in the saw kerf, and *then* tape the pieces together.

Arcs

(See Circles)

Auger Bit

(See Drill Bits)

Awl

The awl, also known as a scratch awl, is a tool that no home workshop should be without. This tool has many uses. It can be used in lieu of a pencil for drawing or scribing lines on wood, plastics, and metals. On darker woods such as mahogany or rosewood, a scribe stands out better than a pencil line.

Check the point of the awl from time to time, especially after using it on metals, to make sure that it is sharp (Illus. 3-16). The awl can be easily sharpened on a belt or disc sander using a fine grit (Illus. 3-17). Be careful, though; don't let it get too hot when sharpening it because it will lose its temper and will not be as effective when scribing metals.

Starting a Hole with an Awl

When drilling into the side of a dowel or other round stock, it is best to use a V block jig and a brad-point drill bit to make a clean hole. However, brad-point bits are not commonly found in a home workshop. If you do not have brad-

Illus. 3-16. Check the point of the awl occasionally to make sure it is sharp.

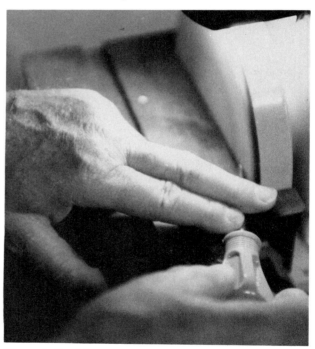

Illus. 3-17. The awl can be sharpened on a belt sander.

point bits, try this method as an alternative solution.

Clamp the ends of the dowel to your drill press table so it lays flat without rolling. Using a mallet, lightly tap the handle of an awl to make a starting hole and then drill slowly into the dowel with a conventional high-speed steel drill bit (Illus. 3-18). Make sure that you clamp your work tightly so that it won't move when you are drilling it.

Illus. 3-18. Drilling into the dowel with a high-speed steel drill bit.

Backsaw

The backsaw, also known as the mitre saw, is generally used in a mitre box. It is also used for cutting tenons, dovetails, and most other wood joints (Illus. 3-19). Al-though its teeth are set for crosscutting, it is used with the grain as well. The heavy spine across the top keeps the saw rigid when being used to make a more accurate cut. Backsaws come in various sizes, but their tooth spacing generally runs between 12 and 14 tpi (teeth per inch). When some types of mitre boxes are used, the spine of the backsaw either slides across or is clamped to an adjustable rail to provide more accuracy.

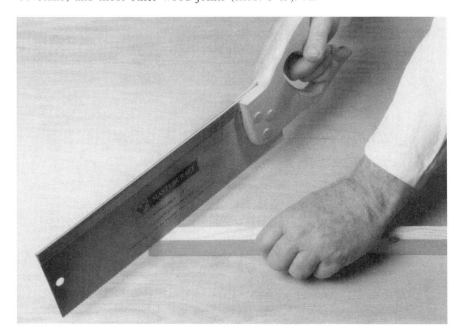

Illus. 3-19. Using a backsaw.

Band Saw

Description of a Band Saw

The band saw is a requirement for any home workshop (Illus. 3-20 and 3-21). Band saws are sized according to the distance between the frame and the blade on the band saw. The common 14-inch band saw will cut material 6 inches thick or more, depending on the manufacturer, and will cut curves and do scrolling. Resawing can be done with the use of a wide blade. Most band saws will accept a fence and a mitre gauge. Most are two-wheel machines, but some, usually benchtop models, have three wheels. Band saws with three wheels make wider cuts, but the blades are more difficult to install and the blade can slip

Illus. 3-21.

off the wheels much more easily. Most saw tables have a tilt feature to allow for mitred cuts. On some band saws, such as the Sears band saws, the saw itself tilts while the table remains horizontal.

Although cutting with a band saw is easy, the cut edges are not as smooth as one would get on a table saw. It is, however, a very versatile tool in that you can replace a blade with a sanding belt, and use a number of different blades for different cuts. Some saws have dual or variable speeds or speed ranges that will allow you to also cut various types of metals. Light aluminum, however, can be cut on a single-speed saw.

Band saws range in price from approximately $150 for a hobby saw to over $2,000 for more elaborate saws. When buying a band saw, make sure that it has a rigid base or stand.

Types of Band-Saw Blade

Band-saw blades come in a multitude of lengths, widths, and tooth counts (Illus. 3-22). They range in width from $3/32$ to 24 inches. The latter can be found at some sawmills. The minimum and maximum blade widths will depend on

Illus. 3-20. A band saw is an essential part of any workshop.

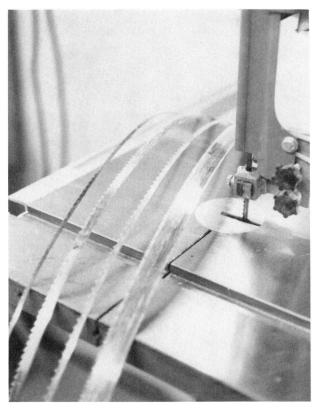

Illus. 3-22. Band-saw blades come in many different lengths, widths, and tooth counts.

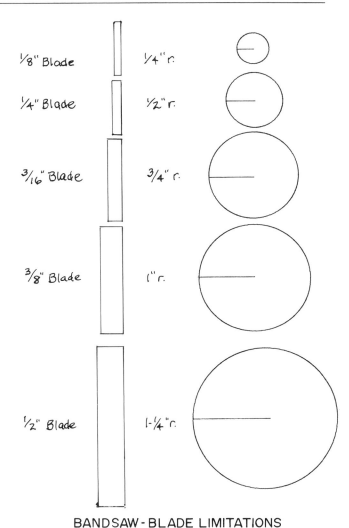

BANDSAW - BLADE LIMITATIONS

Illus. 3-23. The cutting limitations of band-saw blades.

the specifications for your band saw. The type of blade to use will depend on the type of work that has to be done. A narrower blade will cut smaller diameters. A ½- to 1-inch-wide blade will be best for resawing.

Blade lengths also vary, depending on the make and type of saw. If you are buying new blades for a saw which uses a 97-inch-long blade, a 96- or a 98-inch blade will probably work. The blade tension can be adjusted to make up the difference.

The tooth count is another factor. The tooth count is the number of teeth per inch on the blade. The more teeth, the finer and slower the cut. Less teeth will give a faster but rougher cut. A skip-tooth blade is used for ripping. It is best suited for cutting soft metals such as aluminum.

Sizes of Band-Saw Blade

Band saws are great tools for cutting circles, but the radius of the circle to be cut is limited to the width of the blade that you are using (Illus. 3-23). Chart 3-4 indicates the radii certain blade widths will cut. This information will

ensure that you use a blade of the proper width for a specific job, and save you the cost of a new blade, or at least the cost of rewelding. Remember, these are the *minimum radii* that should be attempted with the indicated blade size.

Blade Width	Radius of Cut
⅛ inch	¼ inch
³⁄₁₆ inch	½ inch
¼ inch	¾ inch
⅜ inch	1 inch
½ inch	1¼ inches

Chart 3-4.

Installing Band-Saw Blades

Installing a band-saw blade has always been difficult for me until I discovered the method shown in Illus. 3-24. Place the blade on the top wheel first. Next, using small spring clamps or clothespins, hold the blade secure. Feed it through the guides and over the bottom wheel. Adjust the blade tension, remove the clamps, and check for blade centering. The blade is now installed.

Auxiliary Tables for a Band Saw

An auxiliary table for a band saw, especially a removable one like the one shown in Illus. 3-25, is a great advantage to the woodworker. It is particularly useful for cutting large circles for tabletops, etc.

One way to make an auxiliary table is to laminate two pieces of ¾-inch-thick plywood and screw a piece of aluminum angle to one side. Drill holes into the edge of the saw table casting, and make slots in the aluminum angle to correspond. You can also make a slot for the band-saw table expander pin, and put hinged legs on the table so it can fold up when not in use. It only takes a couple of minutes to set it up with ¼-inch bolts and wing nuts.

The table shown in Illus. 3-26 and Illus. 3-27 is somewhat different and more compact than the first table in that it is cantilevered off the band saw itself. A brace runs from the saw base to a fixed block under the table for stability. Holes are drilled every inch to facilitate a pin for the cutting of circles. Make sure that the holes are in line with the teeth of your most commonly used blade. Make a couple of extra braces of different lengths to support the table at 15, 30, and 45 degrees and mark them accordingly.

Illus. 3-24. An easy method for installing band-saw blades.

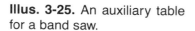

Illus. 3-25. An auxiliary table for a band saw.

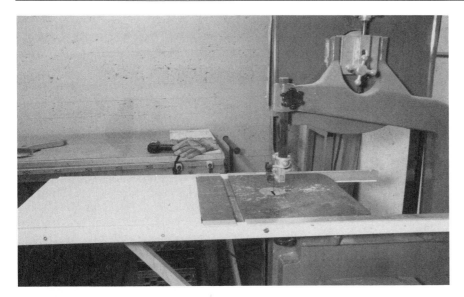

Illus. 3-26 and 3-27. Another auxiliary table for the band saw.

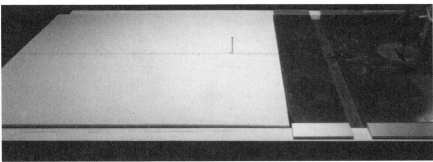

Illus. 3-27.

Cutting Circles on a Band Saw

When cutting large circles such as tabletops on your band saw, use an auxiliary table (see page 36), find the center of your stock, and drill a small hole into it. Start your cut and then drive a nail through the hole and into your auxiliary table. Make sure that the nail is in perfect alignment with the teeth of the saw blade and proceed to cut carefully (Illus. 3-28).

Illus. 3-28. An auxiliary table can be used to cut circles on a band saw.

Cutting Dowels with a Band Saw

To split a short length of dowel with your band saw, cut a V block as shown in Illus. 3-29, set your dowel into it, and carefully push the V block and dowel into the blade. After you have cut about ¾-inch, push a small finishing nail through the kerf to keep the dowel vertical. Now, push only the dowel into the blade.

Illus. 3-29. An easy method for cutting a length of dowel with a band saw.

Another method for cutting or splitting dowels is to square off a piece of scrap and drill a hole in it that is just slightly larger than the dowel (Illus. 3-30). Hold the scrap tightly against the fence and slowly push the dowel through the hole until you have cut about an inch into the dowel.

Now, withdraw the dowel, turn it around and reinsert it into the scrap. Tap a small nail (the size of the kerf) through the stock into the hole. This will keep the dowel from twisting. Continue the cut up to the nail, being careful not to strike the nail with the blade.

Note: Make sure that the dowel that you are splitting is a couple of inches longer than required.

Making Duplicating Cuts with a Band Saw

To make a number of duplicate pattern cuts on your band saw, use double-face tape or rubber cement to hold the desired number of pieces together. Draw your pattern on the top piece and start cutting (Illus. 3-31). After cutting out the shape, don't disassemble the pieces; keep them together to do the edge-sanding. When this is done, simply pry the pieces apart and peel the double-face tape off. If using rubber cement, rub off the residue with your fingers.

Band Saw Rip Fence

I made the band-saw rip fence shown in Illus. 3-32 and 3-33 out of ¾-inch-thick plywood, an aluminum angle

Illus. 3-30. Another method of splitting dowels.

Illus. 3-31. Cutting patterns with a band saw.

Illus. 3-32 and 3-33. A shop-made band-saw rip fence.

Illus. 3-33.

bracket, and a long carriage bolt with a wing nut. Though I had to cut out an area for the blade guard, the fence works well and only took an hour to make. Before ripping, make sure the fence is square to the table.

Sanding with a Band Saw

Most 14-inch band saws will take a blade up to ¾ inch in width. If you buy a roll of sandpaper ¾ inch wide, you can turn your band saw into a belt sander. Cut the abrasive to the length of your band-saw blades (these measurements can be found in your owner's manual). Cut the ends of the abrasive on an angle, much like that on a portable belt sander. Run an approximately two-foot-long strip of fibreglass-reinforced tape along the back of the sandpaper strip, being sure that the tape is as wide as the sandpaper (Illus. 3-34). This tape is usually available at stationery stores. Remove the table insert, guide blocks, bearing guides and guard, install the belt, adjust the tension, and you're ready to sand with the band saw (Illus. 3-35). A 2 × 4-inch piece of scrap clamped to the table behind the belt will help to ensure even sanding on squared pieces.

Making Spiralling Dowels with a Band Saw

Spiralled or fluted dowels are required when making dowelled glue joints because they hold the glue better and thus make a stronger joint. Invariably, however, your tool box or drawer won't have the type or size of dowel required. If you have a fluting tool, you can easily make the type of dowel required. If not, try this technique that I learned a few years ago:

Tilt the table of your band saw 15–20 degrees, use your mitre gauge to hold the dowel at a right angle to the saw blade, and turn on the saw. The amount of pressure that

Illus. 3-35. The band saw ready for sanding.

Illus. 3-36. An easy way to make spiralling dowels with your band saw.

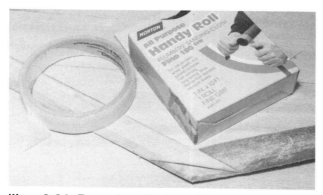

Illus. 3-34. Run a length of masking tape along the back of the sandpaper strip.

you apply towards the blade will determine the depth of the cut. The saw-blade motion will automatically make the spiralling. A little practice and you'll have it down pat (Illus. 3-36).

Belt Sander

Description

The portable belt sander (Illus. 3-37–3-39) is a powerful tool that can be used to smooth rough-cut lumber, to name just one task. Safety should be foremost in your mind when working with this tool. Do not apply pressure to it, as it generally has enough power to do the job at hand. Applying too much pressure will result in gouges in the wood surface.

Belts are available in various grits, the most common being coarse, medium, and fine. This is not a finishing sander, so a fine-grit belt has approximately 80–120 grits.

Most belt sanders now come equipped with dust-collection bags. Make sure the dust-collection bag is emptied often, because it fills up quickly. Some belt sanders have threaded holes on the top so that they may be inverted and bolted down to be used as a fixed belt sander. A fence is sometimes available as an accessory.

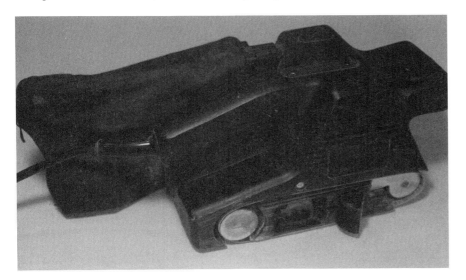

Illus. 3-37–3-39. Belt sanders.

Illus. 3-38.

Illus. 3-39.

Using the Belts

Always loosen the pressure release on your belt sanders after use. Making this a habit will greatly extend the life of your sanding belt. Better yet, remove the belt and store it on a pegboard nested with other belts of the same grit (Illus. 3-40).

Bench Dogs

(Also see Dogs, Workbench Dogs, and Workmate)

Description

I don't know where the term "dog" comes from, but these little tools are dogged in that they are stubbornly persistent in their usefulness on the workbench. Bench dogs are the little dowels or pegs that fit in the holes that are drilled on the workbench (Illus. 3-41). They are extremely useful and versatile. They help you hold your stock when hand-planing, act as a vise to clamp joints, hold stock for sanding, etc.

Making your own bench dogs is easy. Just cut off dowels to the appropriate length.

Blades

(Refer to the appropriate tool)

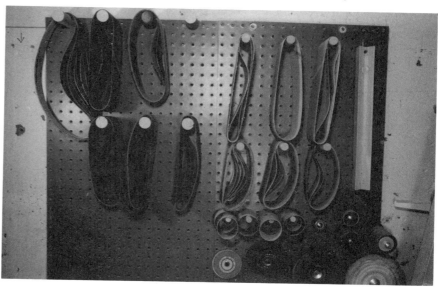

Illus. 3-40. Store belt sander belts on a pegboard with belts of similar grits.

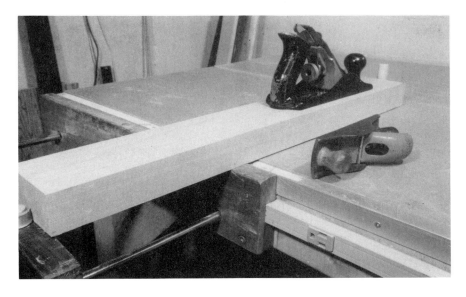

Illus. 3-41. Bench dogs are pegs that fit into the holes that are drilled on the workbench.

Brads

(See Nails)

Buffing Wheel

You can make your own buffing wheels out of old flannel shirts, nightgowns, pajamas, or felt scraps (Illus. 3-42). Cut them 6 or 8 inches in diameter until you have a stack that is about ½ inch thick. Sew them together using the stitching on an old wheel as a guide, and then cut a hole the size of your arbor in the middle of the wheel. Put the arbor washers on both sides and bolt the buffing wheel on tightly. If your arbor can take it, put three or four wheels on to create one wider buffing wheel.

Caulk

Types and Uses

The following are general guidelines concerning what

Illus. 3-42. A shop-made buffing wheel.

type of caulking compound to use and where to use it:

Acrylic caulk should be used on exterior surfaces only. It is sold in a wide range of colors, but it should not be painted. Acrylic has a life exceeding 20 years.

Acrylic latex has interior and exterior applications around windows, doors, wood siding, etc. It can be painted and cleaned up with soap and water.

Butyl®/rubber caulk is used on concrete block, brick, gutters, flashing, chimneys, etc. It may be used below grade and in high-moisture areas. It is available in different colors and can be painted. It has a fairly high shrinkage rate.

Silicone caulk is used on metal, glass, tile, and other nonporous surfaces. It is good for joining dissimilar materials, such as mounting mirrors on walls. It is also very flexible, and will last 20–50 years.

Preventing Caulk from Drying Out

There is nothing more annoying than having the caulk in a previously opened caulking tube dry up. You place the half-full tube in your gun and discover that nothing will come out. The caulk in the nozzle has dried up.

To prevent this, next time you open a tube of caulk and have finished using it, take a large pan-head wood screw, one that is large enough to fit on the inside of the nozzle, and screw it into the nozzle (Illus. 3-44). You can also screw a large electrical wire nut onto the end of the nozzle (Illus. 3-45).

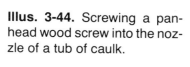

Illus. 3-43. Various types of caulk.

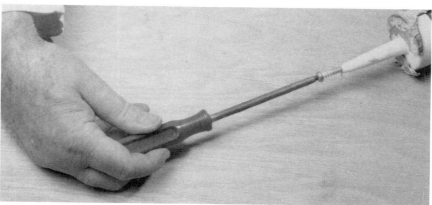

Illus. 3-44. Screwing a pan-head wood screw into the nozzle of a tub of caulk.

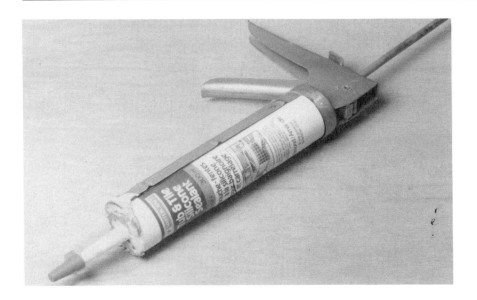

Illus. 3-45. A large electrical wire nut has been screwed onto the end of this caulk nozzle.

Preventing Caulking Tubes from "Running On"

To prevent caulking tubes from "running on" after you have released the trigger, tightly wrap the tube in duct tape before inserting it into the gun (Illus. 3-46). This deters the expansion of the tube that occurs because of the pressure exerted on the back of the tube when the trigger is released. To make doubly sure the tube does not run, also release the trigger catch when releasing the trigger.

Caulking Technique

To do an effective job of caulking around a bathtub, sink, window, or door frame, place a small bead of silicone caulk or other type of caulk around the perimeter (Illus. 3-47). Pour a small amount (about 1 ounce) of dish detergent liquid into a glass or plastic cup along with an equal amount of water. Carefully force the caulk into the corners with your thumb or middle finger, making sure to frequently dip the thumb or middle finger into the liquid.

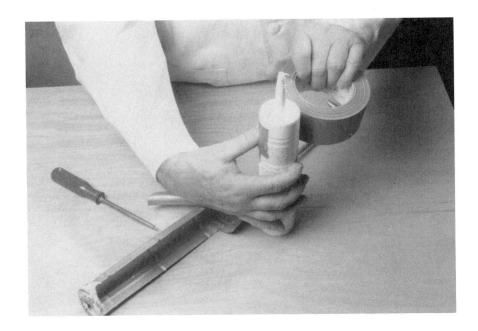

Illus. 3-46. Wrapping duct tape around the caulk tube.

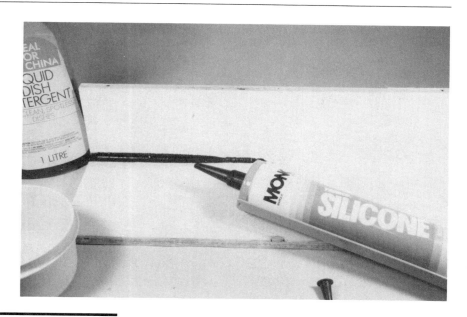

Illus. 3-47. Dip your thumb frequently into a dish of detergent liquid when applying caulk in corners.

Center-Finding

As an example, let's assume that you want to work on a piece of stock that is 5¹³⁄₁₆ inches wide and you have to find the center of it. One way to do this is to cut a 10-inch length of ¾ × ¾-inch stock, make a mark exactly 1 inch from each end and in the exact center of the stock. With your drill press, drill ¼-inch holes into the marks at both ends. Glue a 1¼-inch-long dowel with a ¼-inch diameter into each end. Now, check the diameter of the pencil that you usually use, and drill a hole precisely into the center of the stock.

Now, simply place your pencil in the hole, slide the gauge down the stock, and you have a centerline (Illus. 3-48).

There is another method for finding the centers of stock. Let's assume that you have a board that is 11⅜ inches wide and you want to find its center. Take your builder's square, place the bottom corner of the long side at one edge of the stock, and move it up on an angle until the other edge of the stock joins a whole number, i.e., 14 inches (Illus. 3-49). Then simply divide that whole number by two.

Illus. 3-48. One way of finding the center of stock.

Illus. 3-49. Another method for finding the center of stock.

Chipboard

(See Particleboard and Plywood)

Circles

(Also see Band Saw, Drill Press, Radial Arm Saw, and Table Saw)

Drawing Circles

There will be times when you will want to draw circles and do not have a circle compass available. Here's a simple method for drawing circles up to 24 inches without one. Let's assume that you want to draw an 8-inch radius. With your builder's square, draw a straight line across your stock. Then drive two small nails along the line, 8 inches apart. Lay your builder's square flat on the stock, with the inside corner around the first nail. Put your pencil in the corner of the square and simply move the square and your

pencil up and over to the next nail. This will produce an arc (Illus. 3-50). Repeat the procedure for the next half.

Illus. 3-50. An easy method for drawing circles.

Patterns for Circles

This technique will save you a great deal of time in the future when you want to make circles for wheels, etc. Cut a 12-inch-diameter piece of ¹⁄₃₂-inch-thick polystyrene (see Polystyrene on page 148), and find and mark its center. Draw a line completely up the center (Illus. 3-51). Mark the line exactly every inch from the center to one outer edge. On the other half of the line make a mark every inch, skipping the whole numbers. Start at the ½-inch mark (e.g., ½ inch, 1½ inch, 2½ inch, etc.).

Now, draw an intersecting line completely across the circle and on the left. Mark it every ½ inch. Begin at ¼ inch, and skip the ½ inch and the whole numbers (e.g., ¼ inch, ¾ inch, 1¼ inch, 1¾ inch, etc.). On the right side, make a mark every ¼ inch. Begin at the ⅛-inch mark, eliminating the ¼- and ½-inch marks and the whole numbers (Illus. 3-52).

Drill a ¹⁄₁₆-inch hole at each of these marks, including the center. Drill a ¼-inch hole in a blank space near the top for hanging, sand off the burrs on the back, and, with a felt marker, mark ¹⁄₁₆ inch on that line, etc. Finally, use a compass to draw a circle only at the inch line holes.

To use this device, place it on your workpiece, tap in a finishing nail in the center, put a pencil point in the desired hole, and rotate it. The whole numbers on the jig shown in Illus. 3-52 represent the radii, not the diameters.

Illus. 3-51. Draw a line completely up the center of the pattern.

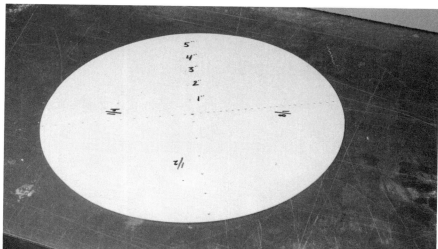

Illus. 3-52. The marked-out pattern.

Circular Saw, Portable

Using a Straightedge

When using a straightedge as a guide for your portable circular saw, you usually have to add the distance from the blade to the edge of the saw shoe to your measurements. If you are a weekend woodworker, you probably have to verify this measurement with a measuring tape each time you use the saw.

To save some time when you use the saw next, write the measurements from both sides of the blade to the shoe edges on the motor housing of your saw (Illus. 3-53). Write these measurements on a sticky label or use a soft-tip marker. Most saw blades cut a ⅛-inch kerf, but make a test cut with your blade and add its kerf measurement on the motor housing with the other measurements.

Proper Cutting Technique

Tear-out or ragged edges won't be a problem on your finished work if, when cutting with your circular saw, you make sure that the good side of your material is always facedown and that you are using the right blade (Illus. 3-54).

Illus. 3-53 (above left). Write the measurements from both sides of the blade to the shoe edges on the motor housing of your saw. **Illus. 3-54 (above right).** When cutting with your circular saw, make sure that the good side of the material is facedown and that you are using the proper blade.

Plywood-Cutting Jig for a Circular Saw

The plywood-cutting jig shown in Illus. 3-55 is made from 2-inch-square aluminum tube and a 1-inch angle. It's about 5 feet long overall, with the tube crosspieces set 48¼ inches apart. It is of proper width so that my portable circular saw can fit snugly in the channels. The jig is perfectly square, so it will fit across the width of a 4 × 8-foot sheet of plywood or similar type of stock.

Set your plywood on two sawhorses, measure for your cut, line up the kerf cut with your mark, lay the jig on top, and put a couple of small wedges in at the bottom. The jig is now ready to be used. To further ensure the accuracy of your cut, you may want to use a couple of clamps on the left side of the jig.

Circular-Saw Blades

(Also see Radial Arm Saw and Table Saw)

Selecting Circular-Saw Blades

One type of circular-saw blade is the carbide-tipped blade.

Illus. 3-55. A plywood-cutting jig for a circular saw.

This blade has a wide range of prices, and can be bought for as little as $5.00. It is much more durable than a high-speed steel blade. Purchase your blade from a reputable dealer. Select only brand-name products.

One basic rule that should govern your blade selection is that the more teeth, the finer the cut. The number of teeth is proportionate to the size of the blade. For example, an 8-inch blade with 35 teeth will give about the same cut as a 10-inch blade with 50 teeth. Some blades, such as planer blades, tend to wobble slightly, and this will affect the cut. Therefore, a set of stabilizers is recommended. These stabilizers are like large washers that are slightly concave and fit on both sides of the blade to stabilize it.

There are also blades, generally 10 or 12 inches in diameter, that have a very shallow cutting tolerance. These blades are very thin for the first 1½ inches or so, and then become thicker up to the arbor hole. These blades are meant for cutting thin materials such as plastic laminates, etc. There is a group of specialty blades that are designed to be used in particular woodworking situations. Included in this group are blades with 200 teeth that are used for plywood and give an extremely smooth cut. Unless you are in the woodworking business and set up for production, they probably won't concern you.

Following are some types of blade that are recommended for use in the workshop (Illus. 3-56). A *combination* blade is a general-purpose blade that will give fairly clean crosscuts and rip cuts. The more teeth it has, the finer the cut. A *crosscut* blade, as its name implies, is the blade best suited for crosscutting. It generally has more teeth to provide a smoother cross-grain cut. A *planing*

blade gives an extremely smooth crosscut, but is very thin and should not be used for ripping or for very thick material. A *rip* blade generally has fewer teeth than other types of blade, because it faces less resistance as it is used to cut with the grain of the wood.

There are special blades for cutting plywood, plastics, laminates, particleboard, Masonite®, nonferrous metals, etc. For information on these types of blade, consult a tool-shop specialist or mail-order catalogues.

Safety Techniques for Blades

Always make sure that there are no teeth or tips missing on your saw blades before starting up your saw (Illus. 3-57). Make it a habit to check, just as you would look out of your rearview mirror before backing up in your car.

One missing tooth usually means that more are loose. If you discover a tooth missing, don't use the blade. A flying carbide tooth can seriously injure you.

Determining the Sharpness of Circular-Saw Blades

The easiest way to determine whether or not your saw blades are sharp is to simply use your thumbnail on the tip of a randomly selected tooth (Illus. 3-58). If the tooth leaves a scratch mark on your thumbnail, the blade is sharp. If it doesn't, have it sharpened.

Never use a dull saw blade. Dull blades can cause excessive strain on your saw's motor and thereby severely shorten its life.

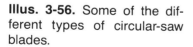

Illus. 3-56. Some of the different types of circular-saw blades.

Illus. 3-57 (above left). Check your circular-saw blades before using them. Make sure that no teeth or tips are missing. **Illus. 3-58 (above right).** To determine whether or not your saw blade is sharp, run your thumbnail on the tip of a tooth. If the tooth leaves a scratch mark on your thumbnail, the blade is sharp.

Fitting Circular-Saw Blades

If you have a circular-saw blade with an arbor hole that is too big for the saw arbor, don't throw it away. Most hardware or tool stores and flea markets carry reducing washers for just this purpose (Illus. 3-59).

Illus. 3-59. This washer will reduce the size of the arbor hole on the blade.

Cleaning Circular-Saw Blades

If your saw blades aren't cutting properly, it may not be because the blade is dull. The blade may just be dirty.

Pine, spruce, and other soft woods are the materials most likely to clog up a blade. They will leave a residue of tar and gum on your blades that will slow down the cutting rate or leave burn marks on your wood. They will also speed up the dulling process on the teeth.

One method of cleaning is to spray on some oven cleaner, and to let the spray sit on a blade for a couple of hours (Illus. 3-60). Another cleaning method is to use Arm and Hammer washing soda (Illus. 3-61).

Check your circular-saw blades often, and keep them clean. The same rule applies to your other blades and bits. Use the same cleaning methods.

One final note: After the blades are clean, give them a shot of silicone spray. This will help retard the buildup of tars, resins, and rust.

Containers for Circular-Saw Blades

Many circular-saw blades come with a plastic container. Save these containers. They are very handy for cleaning blades and for spraying them with silicone (Illus. 3-62).

Illus. 3-60. One method of cleaning circular blades is to spray on oven cleaner and to brush the blades clean.

Illus. 3-61. Another method of cleaning circular-saw blades is to dampen them with washing soda and then brush them clean.

Illus. 3-62. Use the containers for circular-saw blades to clean your blades and to spray them with silicone.

Storing Circular-Saw Blades

The simple storage cabinet shown in Illus. 3-63 was built to store all my 10-inch circular-saw blades. The shelves are made of scrap ³⁄₁₆-inch panelling, while the top, sides, and bottom are made of ½-inch plywood. When putting my blades away, I slip a piece of Styrofoam® packing underneath the blade.

Clamps

Types of Clamps

There are many types of clamps on the market. A partial list would include C-clamps, bar clamps, vises, band clamps, pipe clamps, spring clamps and even clothespins, paper clips, tie wraps. Illus. 3-64 shows some of these clamps.

Shop-Made Framing Clamps

Make your own framing clamps easily and inexpensively by using four cabinet strap hinges (Illus. 3-65). First, bend the tails back to 90 degrees. Next, drill holes in the tails to facilitate ³⁄₁₆- or ¼-inch threaded rod. Use washers and wing nuts on the threaded rod (Illus. 3-66).

Illus. 3-63. A simple storage cabinet for storing circular-saw blades.

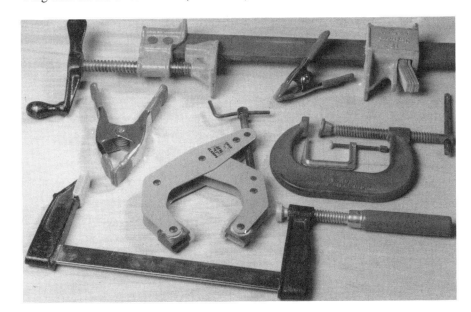

Illus. 3-64. There are many different types of clamps.

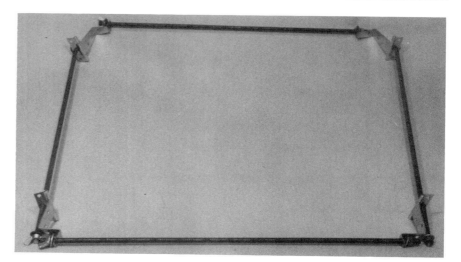

Illus. 3-65. A framing clamp that is shop-made.

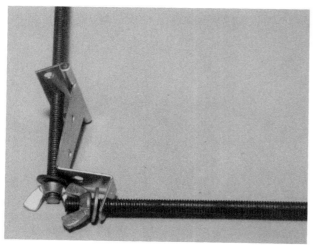

Illus. 3-66. The threaded rod on the framing clamp.

Pipe Clamps

I am sure that there have been times in your workshop when you have wanted to clamp something with pipe clamps that were too short. In preparation for just such an occasion, the next time you are at your neighborhood plumbing shop, pick up half a dozen one-foot lengths of threaded pipe and about the same amount of nipples (couplers) (Illus. 3-67).

Strap Clamps

A nylon web hold-down strap, available at automotive accessory dealers or U-Haul® truck rentals, is the ideal clamp to use for gluing veneer edges to a round surface such as a tabletop (Illus. 3-68). The web strap is also a great clamp for use on loosened chair rungs and legs.

Illus. 3-67. Pipe clamps.

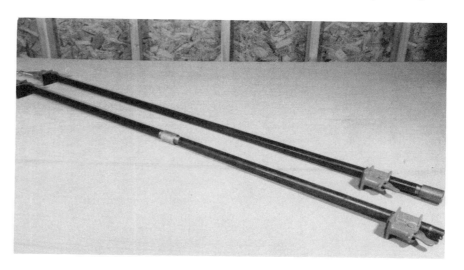

Illus. 3-68. A nylon hold-down strap is ideal to use for gluing veneer edges to a round surface.

Clothespins as Clamps

Looking for a clamp to hold that small project while the glue is drying? Check the laundry room. A spring clothespin is ideal for just this kind of situation (Illus. 3-69).

Tie Wraps as Clamps

A broken chair leg or arm spindle is sometimes difficult to clamp until the glue sets. There are a number of ways to do it, but in most cases the clamp ends up sticking to the workpiece after the glue has dried. One way to prevent this is to use tie wraps instead. Keep a number of tie wraps in different sizes on hand just for such occasions (Illus. 3-70). These tie wraps are made of a nylon material and won't stick after the glue has dried. A pair of wire cutters is all that's needed for removal. Tie wraps are available at most hardware stores, probably in their electrical department.

Clamping Aids

There is a simple technique that will help you hold a project with one hand, slip a piece of scrap wood into the clamp jaws, and tighten the clamp all at the same time. Simply use double-face tape on the wood scraps to adhere them to the clamp jaws (Illus. 3-71 and 3-72). Double-face tape can be found at art supply houses or carpet dealers'.

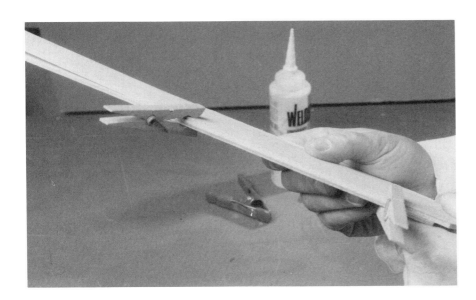

Illus. 3-69. A spring clothespin can be used to hold a small project.

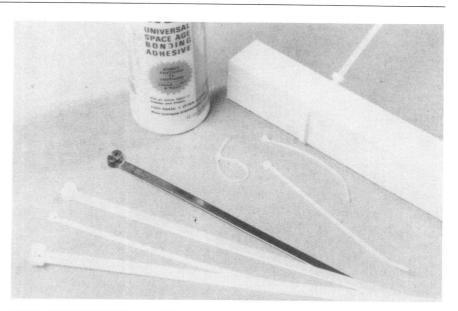

Illus. 3-70. Tie wraps can be used as clamping devices.

Illus. 3-71. Cutting double-face tape to fit on the wood scraps.

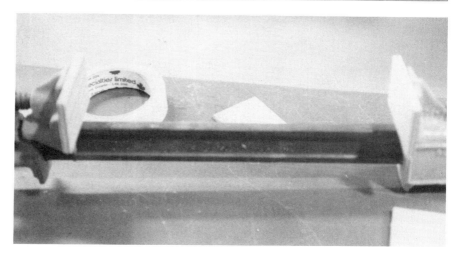

Illus. 3-72. The wood scrap is adhered to the clamp.

Combination Square

To draw precise marks on the workpiece with a combination square, do the following: Drill small (¹⁄₁₆-inch) holes in the center of your combination square scale at precisely the inch lines. Insert your pencil point through one of these holes. (A mechanical or drafting pencil works best.) Then just slide the square along the board (Illus. 3-73).

Compass

Here is a technique for making a compass that will create circles up to 72 inches in diameter. Get hold of a wooden or aluminum yardstick. Drill holes at precisely the top of the 1-inch marks. And at the same position on the width of the ruler, cut a small notch on the ends. Tap a nail into the center of your project. With the ruler notched against the nail, insert a pencil into the desired hole and rotate it (Illus. 3-74).

Illus. 3-73. An easy way of drawing precise marks on wood with a combination square.

Illus. 3-74. With this technique, you can create circles up to 72 inches in diameter.

Coping Saw

(Also see Jigsaw)

The coping saw—also referred to as a fretsaw—is used for fine and delicate cutting of the softer woods (Illus. 3-75).

Countersinking

To countersink for a screw that has to be placed in tight quarters, use a common nail. Hammer its head until it forms a U shape. Put the nail through the screw hole, tighten it in the chuck of your portable electric drill and then pull it towards you until the desired depth is attained (Illus. 3-76).

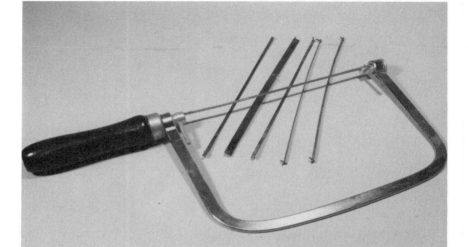

Illus. 3-75. Coping saw.

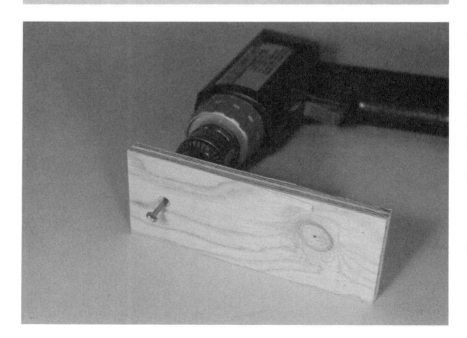

Illus. 3-76. Using a common nail to countersink for a screw.

Curves

(Also see Circles)

Making Freehand Curves

Making freehand curves for scalloped edges, etc., is now an easy task (Illus. 3-77). A flexible curve is available at a reasonable price from most art supply dealers. The flexible curve is made of vinyl, and has material inside that makes it flexible on the horizontal plane and allows it to retain its shape. Get the longest flexible curved (36-inch), if you are making furniture. You'll find it really handy.

Duplicating Curves

Freehand scalloping or decorative scroll work is great if you can make both halves of a piece of work the same. Let's assume, for example, you're making the scalloped back piece for an antique dresser. You have drawn half the pattern freehand and you have to duplicate it for the other half, but can't quite get it right. Do the following: cut the first half on the band saw, cut the scrap off, flip it over, and trace it on the other half of your stock. The pattern will be duplicated precisely (Illus. 3-78).

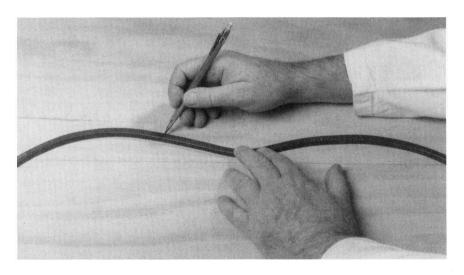

Illus. 3-77. A flexible curve is helpful when you are making freehand curves.

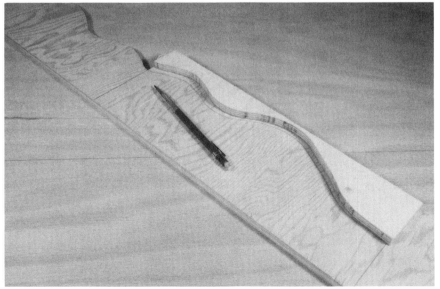

Illus. 3-78. Tracing the pattern on the stock.

Cutting Head

(See Shaper Blades, Shaper Head, and Router)

Dadoes

The traditional way of making a dado is to use dado blades on a table saw. This consists of removing the plate from the table saw, finding the proper blades, and mounting the dado blades on your arbor. This can be cumbersome and confusing.

Now there are wobble dado blades available that make this job much easier. The blade shown in Illus. 3-79 and 3-80 can be adjusted so it will cut ⅛–¹³⁄₁₆ inch. It does leave some arc on the bottom, but this is hardly noticeable.

This wobble dado blade is available with 16, 24 or 32 teeth. There is also a two-blade unit available that is slightly more sophisticated and expensive, but it does the same job.

Illus. 3-79. A wobble dado blade.

Illus. 3-80. Using a wobble dado blade.

Dogs

(See Bench Dogs, Workbench Dogs, and Workmate)

Dowels

Finding the Centers of Dowels

One simple way of finding the center of a dowel is to drill a hole the size of the dowel into a piece of scrap wood. Push the dowel partway into the hole and then, with a wooden mallet, tap a Forstner or brad-point bit into the top of the hole. This will mark the center (Illus. 3-81). The drill bit should be the same size as the dowel.

Another easy way to find the center of a dowel is to use a center finder. This device has a blade set at 45 degrees that cuts a line into the end of the dowel. Hold the dowel tight in the corner, tap it, rotate it 90 degrees, tap again, and you will have located its center. It can also be used for 2 × 2's or smaller pieces of wood.

Veritas® sells a Center Finder (Illus. 3-82). It is available from Lee Valley and other woodworking catalogue suppliers.

Fluting Dowels

You may have been in a situation when you're about to glue up your project, the holes are drilled for the dowels, and you realize that you have no fluted dowels. In such a

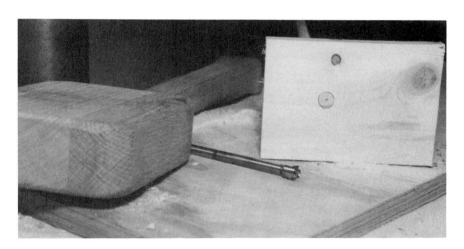

Illus. 3-81. Finding the center of a dowel.

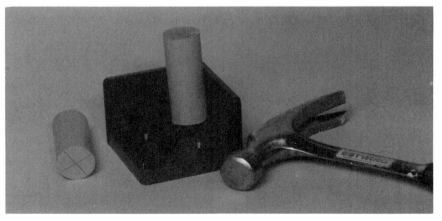

Illus. 3-82. The Center Finder.

case, simply take ordinary dowelling approximately a foot long, find yourself a box wrench that is ⅟₃₂ or ⅟₁₆ inch smaller than the dowel, and, with a wooden mallet, tap the dowel through the wrench (Illus. 3-83). Cut your dowel to size, and you have a fluted dowel ready for use. If you have a pencil sharpener and the dowel will fit into it, slightly sharpen one end (Illus. 3-84). This will make it easier to put it in the hole.

Plugs

There are times when a commercial "hardwood" dowel does not look right when being used as a screw-hole plug. In such a situation, try using a contrasting wood to highlight the plugs (Illus. 3-85). This will work quite well in contemporary furniture.

Another approach is to use a dowel with contrasting layers in it. To make such a dowel, glue the veneer cut-offs until they are sufficiently thick to form a plug. These cut-offs can be of similar or contrasting colors. When they are glued together, use a plug cutter to make the plugs.

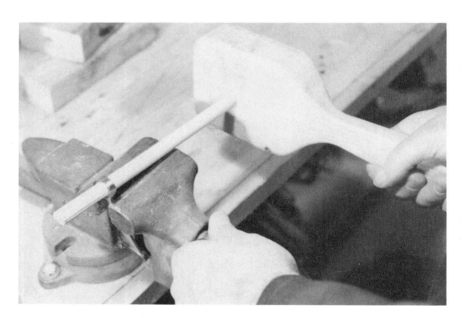

Illus. 3-83. Tapping a dowel through a box wrench.

Illus. 3-84. Sharpening one end of a dowel.

Illus. 3-85. Using contrasting wood to highlight the plugs.

Drawers, Adding Locks to

Drawing Pencils

Young, curious hands always seem to wander into things that they are not supposed to, like a drawer that contains sharp tools. To prevent this, make a lock for the drawer that doesn't look like a lock (Illus. 3-86). Hinge a narrow strip of wood to the bottom front of the drawer so that it drops down just behind the front drawer frame. Drill a finger hole into the dust panel below, so that the lock can be released.

The problem with carpenters' pencils—those round, thick pencils that can leave a mark on virtually any material—is that they are too big, especially when you are marking measurements in increments of $\frac{1}{16}$, $\frac{1}{32}$, or $\frac{1}{64}$ inch. A regular lead pencil always breaks the minute you hit a knot or some cross-grain wood.

A drafting mechanical pencil will prove much more helpful (Illus. 3-87). These pencils are inexpensive and can be bought at an art-supply dealer. The advantage of this type of pencil is that if the lead breaks, you press the

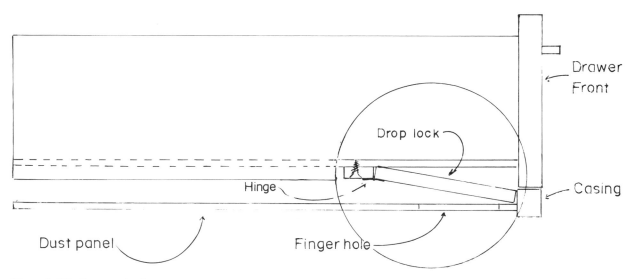

Illus. 3-86. Drawer lock.

Illus. 3-87. Drafting mechanical pencils.

button for more. Also, the lead can be sharpened to a fine point. Buy one with the built-in lead pointer on the top. Also buy a package of "n2" leads. These leads are blacker, stronger, and will stand out better than regular leads when you are making lines on darker woods.

Drill Bits

Types of Drill Bits

An *auger bit* is used in a brace, which is a hand-held drill. It is helical and has a lead screw that makes it easy to start a hole. The shank is usually triangular and tapered so that it won't fit in power drills.

Brad-point bits have a spur on their tips to prevent wandering, especially on odd shapes.

Fly (circle) cutters are expandable bits that are used on a drill press *only*, and only at low speeds. Depending on how the cutter is set, it can cut clean holes or circles. Be extremely careful when using this bit.

Forstner bits are extremely effective bits. They cut very clean holes with very little breakout. A hole partially drilled with a Forstner bit will have a flat bottom.

High-speed steel bits (often abbreviated as hss) are excellent general-purpose drill bits.

Hole saws have serrated edges like a saw blade and are used for cutting larger-diameter holes that are fairly clean.

Self-feed bits are available in larger sizes. They have a lead screw and a bottom cutting blade set on an angle.

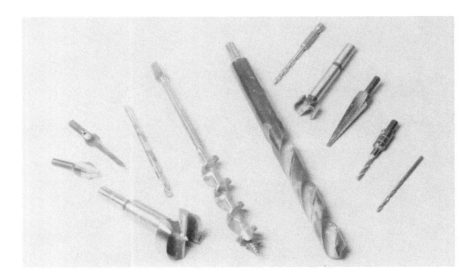

Illus. 3-88. Drill bits.

They cut a clean hole, but must be used with a slow, high-torque drill.

Spade bits are sharp, flat bits. They are used in rougher hole-cutting applications like drilling through studs and joists for wiring and plumbing.

Unibits® are used mainly for drilling into sheet metal, because they are stepped in increments, with each increment being a different diameter.

Note: A drill bit will only drill well if it is well-sharpened.

Using Spade Bits

When using a spade bit for drilling dowel holes, grind down the edges of the bit very slightly (Illus. 3-89). You will find that the dowel will have a tighter fit.

Cleaning Drill Bits

Drill bits tend to accumulate a buildup of tar and gum after extended use. To remove this residue, soak them for approximately 15 minutes in a solution of washing soda and water. Use an old toothbrush to scrub them clean (Illus. 3-90). Wipe them dry and spray them with silicone (Illus. 3-91).

Illus. 3-89. The edges of this spade bit have been grinded down slightly.

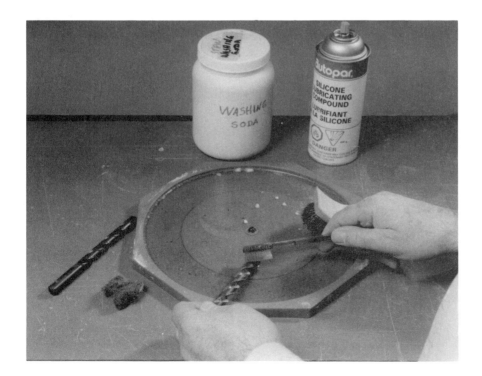

Illus. 3-90. One way of cleaning drill bits is to soak them in a solution of washing soda and water, and then scrub them with an old toothbrush.

Illus. 3-91. Spraying the cleaned bit with silicone.

Drilling

Drill Stops

It's sometimes difficult to determine the depth of your drill hole when using a portable drill, if you don't have any screw-on drill stops handy. Make your own drill stops. Wrap a piece of masking or electrical tape around the bit at the point that you want it to stop (Illus. 3-92), and drill carefully up to where the tape is.

Drilling Holes Through Wood

Whenever you are drilling holes *through* wood, whether you are using a drill press or a portable drill, always keep a piece of scrap wood under your stock (Illus. 3-93–3-95). This will prevent tear-out on the underside of your stock. It's also important to make sure that the scrap piece is placed so that there are no voids or previously drilled holes in the area in which you are drilling the new hole.

Drilling into Metal

When drilling into nonferrous metals, use the slowest speed available on your drill press, and a slow, comfort-

Illus. 3-92. Wrapping a piece of masking tape around the bit.

Illus. 3-93. When drilling holes through wood with a drill press or portable drill, always keep a piece of scrap wood under your stock.

Illus. 3-94. Place the scrap piece so that there are no voids in the area in which you are drilling the new hole.

Illus. 3-95. Drilling into the wood with a portable drill.

able speed on your portable drill. This will be helpful to both yourself and the drill bits. Always clamp your work securely and remove the bit from the work frequently. This will reduce the heat buildup and extend the life of your bits. Always lubricate both the stock and the bit when drilling into metal to keep them cool (Illus. 3-96).

Illus. 3-96. Lubricate both the stock and the bit before drilling into metal.

Drill Press

Checking the Table Level

A drill press will not be effective if the chuck is not perfectly perpendicular to the table (unless, of course, you are angle-drilling). An easy way to true-up your table is to do the following: Take a wire coat hanger and make two 90-degree bends in it so that it is shaped like a Z. Then tighten one end into your chuck. Do *not* turn your drill press on. Lower the shaft until the coat hanger just touches the table (Illus. 3-97). Now, lock the shaft and slowly hand-turn the chuck. If you see a gap between the table and the hanger, adjust your table accordingly.

Circle-Cutting with a Drill Press

To make large holes (up to 8 inches in diameter), use a fly cutter (Illus. 3-98). This tool can be used to cut holes or make wheels. This is achieved by changing the way the cutter is placed in the extension bar.

Be careful when using this tool. Make sure that all adjustment screws are tight and that the tool is tight in the chuck. Set your drill press to its slowest speed and securely clamp your work. *Never use this tool in a portable drill.*

Illus. 3-97. Lock the shaft of the drill press until the coat hanger just touches the table.

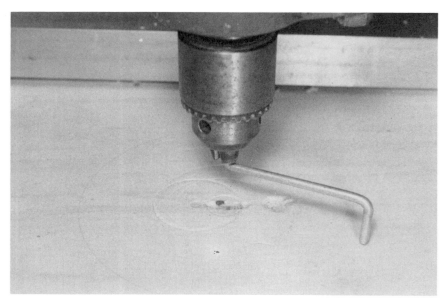

Illus. 3-98. Using a fly cutter to make large holes. Use this tool only in a drill press.

Drilling into Dowels with a Drill Press

Take a piece of wood 2 inches wide, 2 inches thick, and about 12 inches long, and cut a V down the middle of it. Drill a ¼-inch hole on one end. You have made a simple jig for drilling holes into the edge of a dowel, chair leg, etc. (Illus. 3-99). The hole is used to hang the jig on that pegboard right next to the drill press.

Illus. 3-99. Drilling holes into the edge of a dowel.

Drilling the Ends of Dowels

Illus. 3-100 shows a simple jig that can be clamped onto a drill press auxiliary table. To make this jig, take stock

Illus. 3-100. This simple jig will help you use the drill press to drill the ends of dowels.

1¾ × 4 × 8 inches, find its center along its length, and drill a hole with any Forstner bit you have. Other types of drill bits can be used, but the Forstner cuts a cleaner hole. Drill the hole through the stock. After you have marked the center of your dowel end, fit it into the appropriate hole and drill it. If the dowel is too long, swing the table and clamp the jig so that the dowel is off the edge of the table.

Chuck Keys

The chuck key on a drill press can often be hard to locate. One way to solve this problem is to paint it a bright yellow. This will make it easy to spot under all that sawdust.

To make sure that the chuck key will not be misplaced, glue a magnet to it using epoxy (Illus. 3-101). This will make it stick to the drill press housing.

Illus. 3-101. This chuck key is stuck to the drill press with a magnet.

Using a Drill Press as a Lathe

A lathe is not always required to make some simple turnings. A drill press can sometimes be used to do the job (Illus. 3-102).

To use the drill press as a lathe, find the centers on both ends of your stock and mark them. Trim your stock as close as possible to the desired pattern. Drill a ¼-inch hole in the middle of one end and glue a dowel in place, leaving about an inch and a half sticking out. Insert this end into the drill press chuck and tighten it.

Next, take a piece of scrap wood about ½ inch thick and drive a 1-inch nail through it. Put a small washer over the protruding end of the nail. Place this, pointed side up, under the stock, making sure that the nail goes into the center of the stock. Raise your table or lower the chuck to force the nail into the stock. Set your press to its lowest speed and turn it on. If it wobbles, the stock is not centered, so try again. If the scrap is turning, clamp it down.

You're ready to go to work. Use coarse sandpaper strips to get the workpiece to its basic shape and then proceed with progressively finer sandpaper to get the desired finished shape.

Note: *Don't ever try to use lathe chisels in this operation.*

Auxiliary Table and Fence

I made the auxiliary table for my drill press shown in Illus. 3-103 and 3-104 out of ¾-inch-thick plywood and securely bolted it to the base table with carriage bolts, washers, and

Illus. 3-102. Using the drill press as a lathe.

Illus. 3-103. Auxiliary table and fence for the drill press.

Illus. 3-104. Underside of the auxiliary table.

wing nuts. Wing nuts make it easy to remove if I want to do any metal drilling. I can also leave it in place and put another surface under the metal workpiece. I made my table 24 inches wide, but you can make yours to whatever size is needed.

The adjustable fence shown in Illus. 3-103 is made from 2-inch-thick aluminum tubing and an angle that is 1 inch wide and ⅛ inch thick. Although the fence fits tightly, I still use clamps to make sure it doesn't move when I'm using it. I also make sure that it is square to the table before clamping it.

Sanding Wheels with a Drill Press

If you are into toy-making, this technique will expedite the process if your toys require wheels (Illus. 3-105). After your wheels are cut, insert a hex bolt of the required length and diameter through the centers. Use a flat washer between each wheel. Next, lock them on tight with a hex nut, being sure to place a washer between the bolt and the last

wheel. Insert the tail end into the chuck of your drill press and tighten it. Turn your drill press on to a medium speed.

A strip of sandpaper is all that is required to round off the edges. The washers allow you to get between the wheels so that you can do all of the edges in one operation.

Illus. 3-105. Sanding wheels with a drill press.

Drum Sander

You can make your own drum sanders out of various-size dowels (Illus. 3-106). It's really very simple. Drill a ¼-inch hole through dowels that exceed your drill press chuck size, and insert either a carriage bolt and a washer with a nut or a ¼-inch dowel.

Now, cover the largest dowel with sandpaper. To do this, wrap the dowel with double-face tape and then put on the sandpaper. Trim the edges. The drum sander is now ready for use.

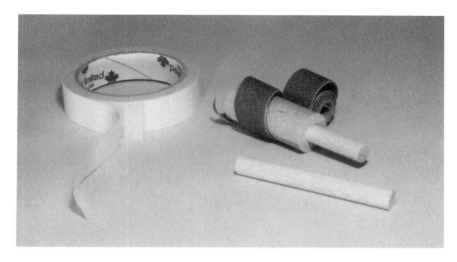

Illus. 3-106. The materials needed to make a drum sander.

Electric Drill

(See Drill Press and Portable Drill)

Epoxy Glue

Mixing Epoxy Glue

Most people squeeze out a blob each of hardener and resin when making a batch of epoxy glue, to approximate a 50/50 mix. Not having the mix in the right proportions can result in a weak glue and reduce its holding power.

An easy solution to get a more accurate mixture is to squeeze a line out of the hardener and then a line of equal length from the resin (Illus. 3-107). Now when you mix them, they will be of equal proportions. Some epoxy glue is packaged in a double-hypodermic container to simplify this.

Another problem sometimes encountered when mixing the hardener and resin is finding a clean, small suitable surface on which to mix them. One solution is to use the bottom of an unopened can of soda (Illus. 3-108). It provides a shallow depression for easy mixing and is heavy enough so that it won't readily tip. Also, on hot days when epoxy tends to set up faster, you can cool the can in the refrigerator first. This will delay the setting.

One final note: When you have finished with the glue, don't set the can down on anything you might need. You might not be able to get the can off.

Illus. 3-107. Squeeze a line of glue from the hardener and then a line of equal length from the resin.

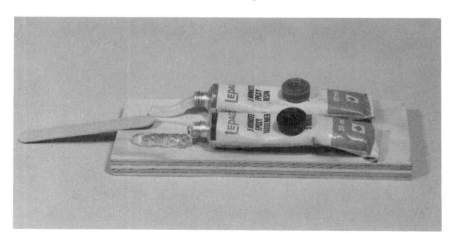

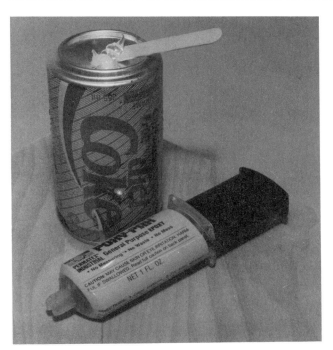

Illus. 3-108. Use the bottom of an unopened can of soda to mix the hardener and resin for the epoxy glue.

Retarding Epoxy Glue Setup

Epoxy resin glue has a tendency to set up (harden) faster in the summer months or in warm climates or locations. To retard this setup time so the glue doesn't harden before you can apply it, fill a mayonnaise jar with ice water, secure the lid, and mix your epoxy glue on the lid (Illus. 3-109).

Extension Cords

Selecting Extension Cords

Care should be taken when using an extension cord for your portable or stationary power tools (Illus. 3-110). Selecting a cord of the wrong length or gauge could put excessive strain on your tool's motor or possibly heat up and burn the wire.

Chart 3-5 indicates the **wire gauge** to be used for the ampere rating of the tool that you are using and the length of the extension cord recommended.

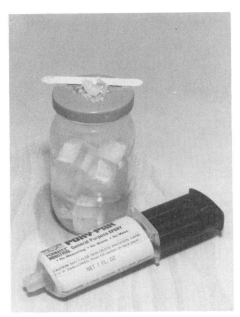

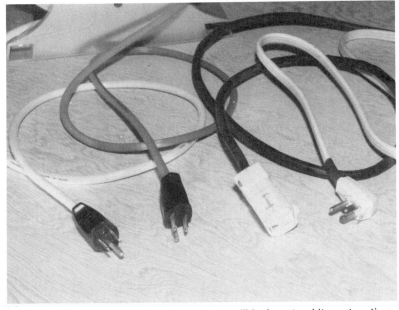

Illus. 3-109 (above left). Mixing epoxy glue on the lid of a jar filled with ice water will help retard its setup time.
Illus. 3-110 (above right). Make sure that you select an extension cord of the proper length or gauge.

Chart 3-5.	CORD LENGTH FEET	AMPERE RATING				
		0–5	10	12	15	20
	25	18 gauge	18 gauge	16 gauge	14 gauge	12 gauge
	50	18 gauge	18 gauge	16 gauge	14 gauge	12 gauge
	75	18 gauge	16 gauge	16 gauge	14 gauge	12 gauge
	100	18 gauge	16 gauge	16 gauge	14 gauge	12 gauge

Storing Extension Cords

Most woodworkers have to rummage through a box or drawer to find that 50- or 100-foot extension cord. Once found, it takes a half-hour or so to disentangle it.

There is an easy way to store extension cords so that they are readily accessible. Drill a hole in the side of a cheap plastic pail, close to its bottom. Make the hole large enough for the plug end of the extension cord to just fit through. With the plug end sticking out of the hole, coil the rest of the wire into the bucket. Plug in the end from the hole and simply reel out the amount of cord needed (Illus. 3-111).

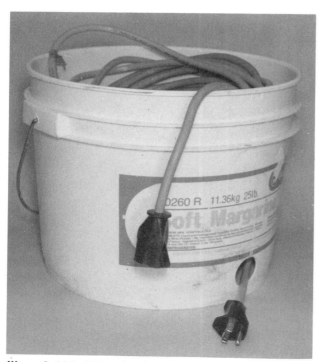

Illus. 3-111. This plastic pail provides an excellent storage bin for long extension cords.

Finishing Nails

You can use the device shown in Illus. 3-112 to put finishing nails in tight corners and other cramped areas of your workpiece. This device is called a brad driver. It's spring-loaded and it works very well. Simply insert your nail into the metal tube (a magnet holds the brad), place the tube where you want your nail to go, and push down hard on the handle. You may still have to use a hammer, especially in hard wood, but at the very least it will start the nail for you.

The brad driver is reasonably priced and available at most hardware or tool-supply stores.

Finishing Wood

Types of Finishing Materials

Shellac is a natural resin that is available in flakes for mixing with alcohol or as a ready mix in either clear (white) or orange. There is very little difference between clear and orange, except that the orange will leave the wood slightly colored, will keep a little longer, and is slightly more resistant to moisture.

Shellac bonds to itself readily and will accept lacquer quite well, though oils and varnish will not adhere to it. It can be polished to almost any sheen, from satin to French polish. It is only used on finishes for interior use and should not be used for bar or counter tops or any surface that is susceptible to alcohol spillage.

Linseed oil is available either raw or boiled. Do not use raw linseed oil. Boiled linseed oil was used for many years

Illus. 3-112. The brad driver can be used to drive finishing nails into tight corners.

because it was cheap and readily available. It leaves a solid, but not too hard, film on wood that is easy to repair, but is not recommended as a final *finish*.

Lacquer is available as a brushing or spraying compound, and has much the same characteristics as shellac. Lacquer is, however, faster-drying, and therefore coats of lacquer can be built up much more quickly. It does take many more coats of lacquer to build it up to a thickness similar to that achieved with shellac or varnish. If you are going to brush it on, use only the very best brushes because it easily leaves brush marks.

Traditional varnish, which is made from natural resins, is now very difficult to get. Today's varnish is much different in that it contains synthetics and hardeners. If it's a hard, durable finish that you want, consider using polyurethane.

Tung oil dries to a harder film than linseed oil and is more moisture-resistant. There seems to be some debate over its usefulness as a final finishing product. I generally reduce it with mineral spirits, apply several coats, and then sand it with 0000 steel wool. This gives it more body and depth.

Sanding sealers are fast-drying solvent release compounds that are used on raw wood to fill in between the raised grain of the wood prior to the application of a finish product. *Do not* use varnish or oils on top of sealers. If the sealer is sanded after it is applied, it will produce a very fine surface. Sealers are excellent for fine-grained woods, but not for open-grained woods such as oak.

Polyurethane (also known as varathane) is a synthetic material that is more properly called a plastic finish. It's available in high-gloss, medium, or satin finishes. Polyurethane is easily applied, dries quickly, and can be used to smooth out brush marks. This is certainly my choice for a durable finish.

There is a relatively new spin-off now on the market that is water-soluble. Different manufacturers sell it under different names. It has an extremely hard and durable finish and dries to the touch in about 15 minutes. Be careful, though: do not use steel wool for sanding between coats of the water-based product. Instead, use a product from 3M called Scotch-Brite®, or Bear-Tex® by Norton. These come in "grits" of varying fineness.

Safety Procedures

Most wood-finishing materials are either flammable or toxic. Extreme care should be exercised when working with them. Never use them near sparks or open flames, and always use an appropriate respirator, one that is rated for toxic fumes or odors. Use these materials only in well-ventilated areas.

There are two very important points that aren't usually addressed on the containers of finishing materials. The first is concerned with the empty containers of these materials. Call your city waste disposal department and they will advise you on how to dispose of these containers. The second point concerns how to dispose of the rags you've been working with. *Never* toss the used rags into a waste bin. *Always* hang them, fully open, up to dry in a cool, well-ventilated area, as, for example, on the clothesline (Illus. 3-114). Used rags left in a pile will spontaneously combust.

There are new laws being passed in both Canada and the United States that will seriously restrict the toxicity and flammability of consumer products such as these. There are a number of wood-finishing products already available that address these concerns. There are water-based contact cement, wood stains, and varnishes on the market now that are safer to use than the older materials.

Illus. 3-113. Finishing products.

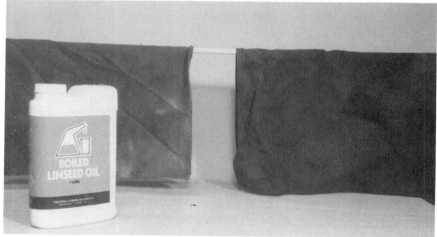

Illus. 3-114. Always hang used rags up to dry in a cool, well-ventilated area.

Finishing Techniques

For a beautiful satin finish, I use a satin polyurethane. I give the surface at least three coats and sand in between each coat (Illus. 3-115). Two or three days after the final coat has dried, I apply boiled linseed oil to the surface (just a little) by rubbing it in circular motions with 0000 steel wool (Illus. 3-116). After this is done, I wipe it down with a soft cloth moistened with paint thinner, then wipe it dry. *Note:* Do not use this method between coats if you are using water-soluble polyurethane (varathane). To sand between coats of this product, use a fine grade of Bear-Tex® or Scotch-Brite® abrasive pads.

Illus. 3-115 (right). To create a beautiful satin finish, first apply at least three coats of polyurethane to the surface. Sand in between each coat.

Illus. 3-116. Next, apply boiled linseed oil to the surface. Rub it in in circular motions with 0000 steel wool.

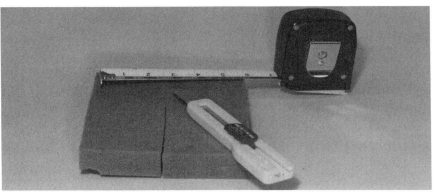

Illus. 3-117. Materials for cutting foam.

Fly Cutter

(See Drill Bits)

Fretsaw

(See Coping Saw and Scroll Saw)

Foam

(Also see Styrofoam®)

Cutting Foam

There are times when you will have to cut foam, such as when you are cutting it to fit an exact shape for packing or upholstering. To make the foam easier to cut, place it in your freezer for about 12 hours prior to cutting it. It will be much easier to cut and there will be less mess (Illus. 3-117).

Funnels, Making

You can never find a funnel when you need one. Here's an easy and quick solution for making one. Simply cut the top off of a two-litre plastic bottle of soda, carefully on a band saw or by using a utility knife (Illus. 3-118 and 3-119). Make the cut 3–4 inches below the top. While you're at it, cut several bottles and keep them near your paint.

Illus. 3-118 and 3-119. Cutting the top off a plastic bottle of soda. This is an easy way to make a funnel.

Illus. 3-119.

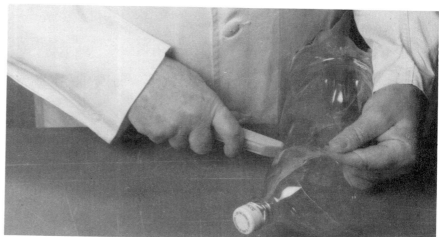

If you want to hang the funnels up, drill a hole in one side just below where you are going to cut the plastic bottle, and then cut the bottle. Don't throw away the caps on the soda bottles. The funnels make good mixing containers as well, so the caps can be used to add ingredients to the funnel.

Furniture, Heights

Ceiling:	96 inches
Door:	80 inches
Bar:	42 inches
Kitchen Counter:	36 inches
Workbench:	33 inches
Kitchen Table, Dining Table, and Desk:	29 inches
Typing Table and Word Processor:	26 inches
Bar Stool and End Table:	24 inches
Dining and Kitchen Chair Seats:	18 inches
Sofa Seat and Easy Chair Seats:	16 inches
Coffee Table:	14 inches

Chart 3- 6.

Chart 3-6 and Illus. 3-120 indicate the acceptable heights for various items of residential furniture.

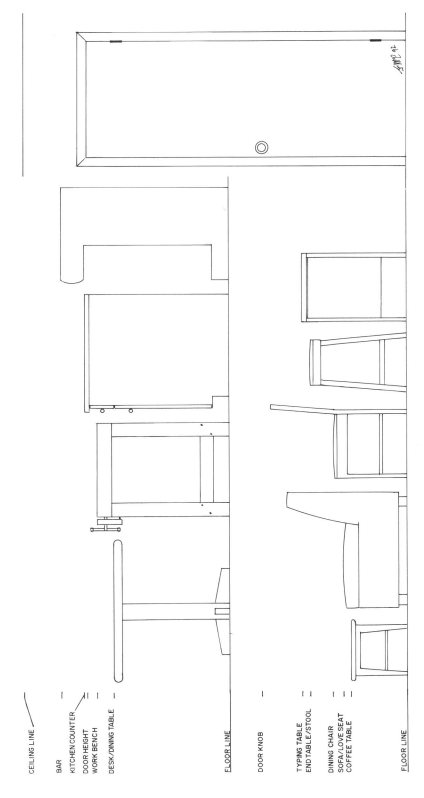

CEILING LINE

BAR
KITCHEN COUNTER
DOOR HEIGHT
WORK BENCH
DESK/DINING TABLE

FLOOR LINE

DOOR KNOB

TYPING TABLE
END TABLE/STOOL

DINING CHAIR
SOFA/LOVE SEAT
COFFEE TABLE

FLOOR LINE

Illus. 3-120. Relationship of heights of various pieces of furniture.

Glass, Cutting Circles in

To cut small circles in clear glass or a mirror, secure a conventional glass cutter into your fly cutter and install these cutters into your drill press (Illus. 3-121). Put a piece of felt cloth on the table, with your stock on top of it. Carefully clamp the stock to the table.

Now, set your drill press to its slowest speed and very, very gently, lower the blade onto the glass so that is *just* scribes the surface. Using the chipper on the cutter, start chipping away at material around the scribed circle. Though in the movies thieves are shown easily cutting circles freehand with a glass cutter and suction cup, in real life this isn't how it is done.

Glue

(Also see Adhesives and Epoxy Glue)

Alternatives to Glue

Double-faced tape, which is readily available at most art-supply or carpet-supply dealers, can often be used as a substitute for glue. If you are not able to find any, substitute a couple of drops of hot melt glue, or use rubber cement on only one of the two mating surfaces (Illus. 3-122).

Protecting the Finish from Glue

Before gluing your project together, try lightly rubbing a wax candle on the edges where glue may ooze out and

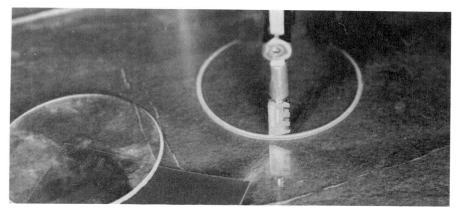

Illus. 3-121. Cutting small circles in glass.

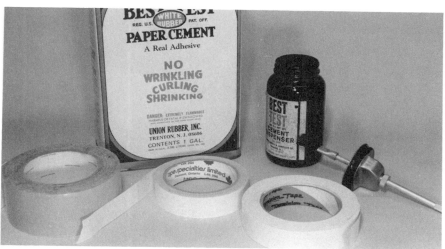

Illus. 3-122. Double-faced tape, hot-melt glue, and rubber cement can all be used as adhesives.

stain your finish (Illus. 3-123). The dried glue should just peel off, and a light sanding will remove any traces of the wax.

Spreading Glue

One method of spreading white glue on larger surfaces is to use a printer's brayer (Illus. 3-124). These are normally used for spreading printer's ink, but they work very well with white glue as well. They come in various sizes and are available at art-supply stores. Wash the printer's brayer off in warm water after use.

Another method of spreading glue is to use a glue spreader (Illus. 3-125). These are inexpensive and available at both flooring or ceramic tile dealers. Get the type of glue spreader with the most and the shallowest notches. Rinse it in warm water after using white glue, or with a suitable solvent if using other types of glue.

Glue can also be spread with old hacksaw blades (Illus. 3-126). Carefully break one in half. Cut 6 inches or so off an old broom handle. Saw a slot on the end of it on your band saw, mix up some epoxy glue, and glue the top edge of the hacksaw into the slot. The result is an effective glue spreader.

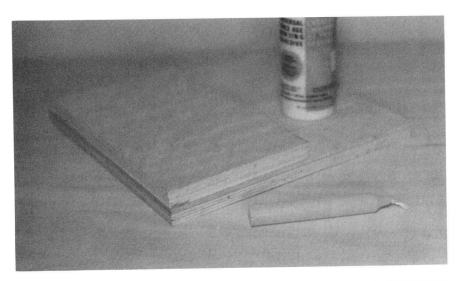

Illus. 3-123. Lightly rubbing a wax candle on the edges of a project will help protect the project finish from glue.

Illus. 3-124. A printer's brayer can be used to spread white glue on larger surfaces.

Illus. 3-125. A glue spreader.

Illus. 3-126. Another method of spreading glue is to use an old hacksaw blade.

Gluing Racks

You can fit scrap pieces of 2 × 4 stock over your sawhorses to make a gluing rack (Illus. 3-127). The slots on the bottom of the gluing rack should be cut so that they fit snugly on top of your sawhorse (Illus. 3-128). The upper slots will hold your bar or pipe clamps, depending on the cut. The big advantage of this gluing rack is that it will not take up space on your workbench while you are waiting for glue to dry.

Grease

(See Lubricants)

Hand Tools

Mending the Handles of Hand Tools

Hand tools like pliers, wire cutters, etc., are bought with plastic-coated grips. After a lot of use, these grips either break or wear off. Here's an easy way to replace them. Cut heat-shrink tubing, available by the foot at most electrical supply shops in various colors and sizes, to the size of your particular handle(s). Now, keep a hair dryer or a heat gun nearby, ready for use. Coat the handle(s) with contact cement and, while the glue is still wet, slip on the heat-

Illus. 3-127. A shop-made gluing rack.

Illus. 3-128. Fit the slots on the bottom of the sawhorse gluing rack so that they fit over the sawhorse.

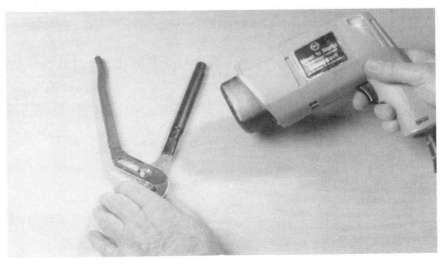

Illus. 3-129. Mending the handle on a pair of pliers with heat-shrink tubing and a heat gun.

shrink tubing and dry the glue with the hair dryer (Illus. 3-129). The result is new handle grips.

Another way of mending the handles of your hand tools is by dipping them in a product called Color Guard®, made by Locktite (Illus. 3-130). This is a thick-liquid, rubbery material that semi-hardens. It softens the grips on the tools. Color Guard is available in about six colors, so it makes tools easily identifiable.

Illus. 3-130. Color Guard® can also be used to mend the handles of tools.

Preserving Hand Tools

You can preserve your hand tools and keep them rust-free by using a product called Rust Check® (Illus. 3-131). Rust Check prevents rust from forming. It is used by automobile dealers, and they should be willing to sell you or maybe even give you some.

A plastic spray bottle makes Rust Check easy to apply. To use it, soak your (metal) hand tools in it for a couple of days, and then wipe them off. Repeat once a year.

Hardboard, Uses and Characteristics

Hardboard, a generic name for what is often called Masonite®, is made from wood chips that are bonded together under high pressure and heat and formed into sheets of various thicknesses (Illus. 3-132). Hardboard is usually available in thicknesses of $1/8$, $3/16$, $1/4$, $3/8$, $1/2$, and $3/4$ inch. The sheets are usually made in 4×8-foot sizes, but are also available in 5-foot width and in lengths of 10 and 12 feet, etc.

Illus. 3-131. Use Rust Check® on your tools to prevent rust from forming.

Illus. 3-132. Hardboard is available in different thicknesses and finishes.

As there is no grain to contend with, hardboard will be equally strong in either direction, and it may be nailed, glued, and screwed. Hardboard may be cut with conventional hand or power tools, but carbide-tipped blades are best.

The sheets are readily available as smooth on one side (S1S) or on both sides (S2S). Sheets that are smooth on both sides are also available patterned, embossed, grooved, striated, tiled, or perforated. Perforated sheets are known as pegboard.

Tempered hardboard is a much harder and more rigid material that has been given an additional treatment. It is available in all the same dimensions as standard hardboard, and is also available patterned. When purchasing hardboard, specify standard or tempered.

Hardboard is used for drawer bottoms, cabinet backs, and as core materials for veneers and laminates. Both standard and tempered hardboard may be used indoors, but only tempered hardboard should be used outside or in damp areas. Hardboard is available in a number of patterns and textures that may be used as exterior siding material.

The information on hardboard presented in this section has been supplied courtesy of Canadian Pacific Forest Products limited, Canexel Hardboard Division.

Hardwood

Definition

Hardwood refers to wood such as oak, maple, walnut, etc. Softwood refers to wood such as pine, spruce, etc.

Hardwood Board Foot Chart

To determine the quantity of board feet in a piece of dimensioned lumber or hardwood, find the dimensions in Chart 3–7, and then multiply the length of that dimension by the factor number. For example, if you want a 2 × 4-inch piece of wood that is 8 feet long, multiply 8 by the factor in the chart opposite 2 inches thick and 4 inches wide. This factor is 0.667, so you would multiply 8 feet × 0.667 to arrive at 5.3 board feet (Illus. 3-133).

	THICKNESS	WIDTH	FACTOR
	1″	2″	0.167
	1″	3″	0.25
	1″	4″	0.333
	1″	5″	0.147
	1″	6″	0.5
	1″	8″	0.667
	1″	10″	0.833
	1″	12″	1.0
Chart 3-7.	1¼″	4″	0.417
	1¼″	6″	0.625
	1¼″	8″	0.833
	1¼″	10″	1.041
	1¼″	12″	1.25
	2″	2″	0.333
	2″	4″	0.667
	2″	6″	1.0
	2″	8″	1.333
	2″	10″	1.667
	2″	12″	2.0

Illus. 3-133.

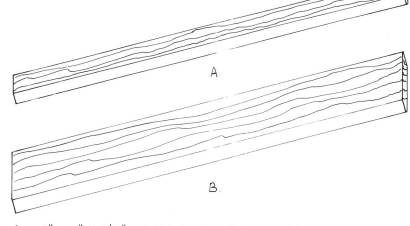

A = 2″ X 4″ X 8′0″ = 8 X 0.667 or 5.3 Board feet.
B = 2″ X 10″ X 8′0″ = 8 X 1.667 or 13.336 Board feet.

Hardwood Designations

Chart 3-8 lists the designations given when ordering hardwood, and the nominal (described) thickness of each designation. It was supplied by the Canadian Wood Council.

Chart 3-9 provides information on sizes, standard grades, and cutting requirements for hardwood. It was provided courtesy of the Canadian Wood Council.

NAME	NOMINAL THICKNESS
Board	1–2 inches
Four-quarter (4/4)	1 inch
Five-quarter (5/4)	1¼ inches
Six-quarter (6/4)	1½ inches
Eight-quarter (8/4)	2 inches
Plank	3 inches or more
Timber or post	3 inches square or more.

Chart 3-8.

GRADES AND CUTTING REQUIREMENTS

Hardwood lumber is graded according to NHLA *Rules* to evaluate the quantity of clear or usable wood in each piece, based on cutting requirements (Table 2). This method assumes that the lumber will be further sawn to lengths and widths, so that knots and other characteristics can be removed. Hardwoods are usually graded on the poorer side of the board.

The top grades of hardwood lumber contain high percentages of clear or knot-free wood in relatively long, wide cuttings; however, no grade calls for completely clear lumber. The top grades are "Firsts and Seconds", usually marketed together as one grade and often marketed with the next lower grade, Selects, as "Selects and Better". These grades are sometimes sold with yet a lower grade, No. 1 Common, as "No. 1 Common and Better". No. 1 Common yields a minimum of about 65% clear cuttings (compared with about 80% for Firsts and Seconds).

Generally, the upper grades should only be specified for applications where appearance is critical. Knots and other characteristics may be acceptable in some locations. It may be most economical to order a larger quantity of lower grade material to obtain an equal amount of clear-face cuttings, if long cuttings are not a requisite.

No. 2 Common grade can be used for a variety of applications. Typical uses are for furniture and flooring; occasional uses are for pallets and containers. Generally, No. 2 Common yields a minimum of 50% clear-face cuttings, and even more if only small clear pieces are needed.

No. 3A Common allows pieces yielding one third clear-face cuttings with no limit to the number of cuttings. No. 3B Common admits pieces yielding 25% sound cuttings. These grades are frequently used in pallets or frame stock for upholstered furniture.

The proportion of hardwood grades varies from mill to mill, depending on log quality. The upper grades of No. 1 Common and Better, however, are normally about a third to one half of mill production. The user can economize by selecting grades wisely. One should determine average width, length and percentage of pieces longer than 12 feet for higher grades before ordering.

Chart 3-9 (here and page 88 and 89).

Hardwood lumber is graded in the rough and is not grade marked unless specifically requested. For a large order, the buyer can engage an independent NHLA grader to undertake a grade inspection, and provide a certificate. It is usually sufficient to specify the desired grade or grade combination.

There are special grading rules for some species, such as walnut and butternut, in the standard grading rules. There are also special product grades, such as "hardwoods for construction" (blocking, planking, mine lumber and sheet piling).

CUTTING SIZES

Hardwood lumber is normally sold in rough form, within given manufacturing tolerances (Table 3). Surfaced lumber is also subject to tolerances; the manufacturer can provide details. Widths and lengths are generally random, but are related to grades through the cutting unit and minimum grade requirements. Thus, the desired size can affect grade selection as much as aesthetic factors.

Certain products have preferred sizes and lengths. Pallet stock is sometimes cut about 24, 40 and 48 inches long, with specified widths and thicknesses. Precut sizes eliminate waste at the pallet factory. The mill can usually find a use for its waste materials, such as for pulp chips.

MOISTURE CONTENT

Some hardwood lumber is kiln-dried at the lumber mill or by custom kiln driers or users prior to use. In some other cases, mills may be integrated with secondary manufacturers, such as flooring mills, that do their own kiln-drying. Moisture content should be specified by the buyer. Most low-grade pallet stock is shipped green for economic reasons.

For many applications, hardwood lumber is kiln-dried to about 6 to 8%, which is the average equilibrium moisture content indoors in most Canadian climates. After drying, the lumber is stored in a protected area at the kiln, or shipped directly to the user. Under normal conditions of transport, the outer portion of some boards may pick up moisture, but this should be quickly lost indoors.

Generally, a charge of lumber can be expected to down grade during kiln drying (from 5 to 10%). Beech particularly is susceptible to warping and checking during kiln drying.

To avoid staining during warm and humid weather and to aid drying, undried lumber should be stacked in well-spaced piles, preferably with "stickers" (narrow strips of hardwood) between layers. Stickers are removed immediately after drying, although some stickers are left in the pile, at least every 10 inches in depth, for ventilation. If stickers are too wide, they can impede drying and lead to staining where they are in contact with lumber. The proper size is $3/4$ by $1 1/2$ inches, kiln dried prior to use. Anti-stain treatments are sometimes applied to the lumber before drying.

Hardwood lumber can be end-coated to prevent excessive end-checking, using proprietary materials, or paraffin with a minimum melting point of 140°F. Unless preventative measures are taken, end checks can develop into end splits, lowering the lumber grade. Red oak is particularly vulnerable to end checking, especially if it is dried unevenly or too rapidly.

Little shrinkage occurs unless the lumber is green or partly air-dried. Contracts for green lumber should have shrinkage allowances (Table 3).

The "Standard Kiln Dried Rule" in the NHLA Rules states that the grade and measurement of lumber before kiln-drying shall be the basis of the seller's invoice. Inspection could be ordered after lumber has been kiln-dried, however, in which case buyer and seller should agree upon an allowance for shrinkage in the total measurement (5 to 8% depending on species). The "Standard Kiln Dried Rule" gives allowances for scant thicknesses and widths. Checks and warp are not considered defects. A "Special Kiln Dried Rule" allows kiln-dried lumber to be graded and measured as such on the seller's invoice, with the same restrictions on checks and warp as for green or air-dried lumber.

TABLE 2 Standard Grades and Cutting Requirements

Grades	Firsts	Seconds	Selects	No. 1 Common	No. 2 Common
Cutting Requirements	Widths: 6'' and wider Lengths: 8 to 16 feet *S.M. % Clear Face Cuts 4' to 9' 91²/₃ 1 10' to 14' 91²/₃ 2 15 and up 91²/₃ 3	Widths: 6'' and wider Lengths: 8 to 16 feet *S.M. % Clear Face Cuts 4' and 5' 83¹/₃ 1 6' and 7' 83¹/₃ 1 8' to 11' 83¹/₃ 2 12' to 15' 83¹/₃ 3 16' and up 83¹/₃ 4 6' to 15' S.M. will admit 1 additional cut to yield 91²/₃% Clear Face. **	Widths: 4'' and wider Lengths: 6 to 16 feet *S.M. % Clear Face Cuts 2' and 3' 91²/₃ 1 Reverse side cutting sound or not below No. 1 Common. 4' and over shall grade on one face as required in Seconds with reverse side of board not below No. 1 Common or reverse side of cuttings sound. See Rule (Par. 70) defining edges of boards 4'' and 5'' wide.	Widths: 3'' and wider Lengths: 4 to 16 feet *S.M. % Clear Face Cuts 1' Clear 2' 75 1 3' and 4' 66²/₃ 1 5' to 7' 66²/₃ 2 8' to 10' 66²/₃ 3 11' to 13' 66²/₃ 4 14' and up 66²/₃ 5 3' to 7' S.M. will admit 1 additional cut to yield 75% Clear Face.	Widths: 3'' and wider Lengths: 4 to 16 feet *S.M. % Clear Face Cuts 1' 66²/₃ 1 2' and 3' 50 1 4' and 5' 50 2 6' and 7' 50 3 8' and 9' 50 4 10' and 11' 50 5 12' and 13' 50 6 14' and up 50 7 2' to 7' S.M. will admit 1 additional cut to yield 66²/₃% Clear Face.
Minimum Cutting	4'' x 5' or 3'' x 7'			4'' x 2' or 3'' x 3'	3'' x 2'

Notes: *Surface measure.
  **Admits also pieces 6'' to 9'' wide of 6' to 12' surface measure that will yield 97% in two clear-face cuttings of any length, full width of the board.
Source: National Hardwood Lumber Association Rules
  National Hardwood Lumber Association
  Box 34518
  Memphis, TN, USA 38134

Chart 3-9 continued.

TABLE 3 Hardwood Lumber Sizes

Dimension	Rough Sizes (Standard)	Shrinkage Allowance (Kiln-Dried Lumber)	Allowance for Surfaced Sizes	Tolerances
Thickness (Specified in Inches, or in Fractions: $4/4''$, $5/4''$, $6/4''$, $7/4''$, etc.)	$3/8'' - 1''$, increments of $1/8''$ $1'' - 2''$, increments of $1/4''$ $2'' - 6''$, increments of $1/2''$ Rough lumber having greater variations than tolerances in last column is measured for thickness at thinnest cutting and classed miscut. Special tolerances are allowed for "hit or miss" lumber.	Allow about $1/32''$ for each inch of thickness. Contracts for green lumber should specify dimensions required to provide for shrinkage allowance. Ten % of a shipment of dry quartered lumber can be $1/16''$ scant on one edge if other edge is full thickness ($1/8''$ scant for $2''$ and thicker lumber); this is not included in measurement of tolerances.	For kiln-dried lumber, surfaced two sides (S2S), allow: $3/16''$ for thicknesses of $3/8''$ to $1 1/2''$ $1/4''$ for thicknesses of $1 3/4''$ to $4''$ (Note: S1S lumber is subject to special contract).	Maximum variation, except for wane, is $1/8''$ for thickness of $1/2''$ or less $3/16''$ for thicknesses of $5/8''$ and $3/4''$ $1/4''$ for thicknesses of $4/4''$ to $7/4''$ $3/8''$ for thicknesses of $2''$ to $3 1/2''$ $5/8''$ for thicknesses of $4''$ to $6''$
Width (Specified in Inches)	Standard sizes depend on end use. Hardwoods are often shipped random-width, and minimum widths depend on grades. Allowance must be made for edge-jointing and waste in flooring.	Allow about $1/16''$ for each inch of widths. Contracts for green lumber should specify dimensions required to provide for shrinkage allowance.	If widths are specified, and lumber is surfaced one edge (S1E) or two edges (S2E), allow $3/8''$ for lumber less than $8''$ wide, and $1/2''$ for lumber $8''$ and wider. Surfaced sizes could be subject to contract.	Shipment of stock widths or specified widths must be at least 90% full widths; 10% can be up to $1/4''$ scant in width (except for sill stock).
Length (Specified in Feet)	Standard lengths depend on end use, but are generally $4'$ to $16'$ inclusive. Even lengths (4, 6, 8, etc.) should make up at least 50% of a shipment. Bundles include pieces up to $6''$ over and $6''$ under standard lengths.	None (wood shrinks very little lengthwise)	None (lengths are not surfaced).	Percentages of short lengths are defined in rules for specified grades; if an average length or percentage of lengths is required, the contract should so specify.

Chart 3-9 continued.

Types of Hardwood

Following is a list of the various types of hardwood according to their commercial names and, in parentheses, their common tree names.

Alder (red)
Ash (black, blue, green, Oregon, pumpkin, and white)
Aspen
Basswood (American)
Beech (American)
Birch (Alaska paper, grey, river, sweet, and yellow)
Buckeye (yellow)
Butternut
Cherry (black)
Cottonwood (balsam poplar, black, Eastern)
Ebony
Elm (American and cedar)
Hackberry
Hickory, pecan
Hickory, true (mockernut, pignut, shagbark, shellbark)
Holly, American
Honey locust
Locust (black)
Madrone (pacific)
Magnolia (cucumber tree, Southern, sweetbay)
Mahogany (African)
Maple (bigleaf and black)
Maple, red, (silver, striped, and sugar)
Oak, red (black, laurel, Northern red, pin, scarlet, Southern red, water, willow, bigtooth, quaking)
Oak, white (bur, chestnut, live, overcup, post, swamp chestnut, white)

Persimmon (common)
Rosewood (African and Brazilian)
Sassafras (sweetgum)
Sycamore (American)
Teak (African and Honduras)
Tamoak
Tupelo (black and water)
Walnut (black)
Wenge
Willow (black)
Zebrawood

Holes

(Also see Drill Press and Portable Drill)

Enlarging Holes

To enlarge a hole that you have already drilled, find a dowel or a square piece of scrap that is the size of the drilled hole. Find the center of it and then cut it off to the thickness of your workpiece. Insert it into the hole and then proceed to drill with the correct size bit (Illus. 3-134). Make sure that your workpiece is well secured to your table.

Hole Saw, Description and Uses

There are two types of hole saw. The first is a handsaw with a pointed, tapered blade that is called a hole saw and it is used for cutting into plasterboard, panelling, etc., to make holes for plugs and switches. Your tool box should include this.

The second type of hole saw are power-driven saws that make circles (Illus. 3-135). These saws are described in this section.

Hole saws are very helpful to toy makers because they do a great job of cutting wheels. They can be purchased separately or in sets. Sets of hole saws are more economical because they are usually sold with only one mandrel.

If you are using the hole saw in a portable drill, you must use it with the pilot bit, which, of course, will leave a ¼-inch hole in the middle. If you are using a drill press, clamp your material securely. You do not have to use the pilot bit. Whichever method you use, do so with the slowest speed on your machine.

Illus. 3-134. Enlarging a drilled hole.

Illus. 3-135. The parts of a hole saw.

One technique that prevents the wheel from sticking inside the bit is to keep raising and lowering the drill into the workpiece, especially when you get close to the end. Before it does get to the end, however, turn the workpiece over and drill from the other side. This won't be so easy if you are not using the pilot bit, but it can still be done if you are using a fence on your drill press.

Jigs, Sanding

When building the wooden jigs described in this book, be sure to sand them smooth with a palm or orbital sander. Sand all the sides and put a slight chamfer on the edges. Believe me when I say that this little extra effort will prevent much discomfort later on. Splinters hurt going in, but hurt even more when pulled out.

Joints, Glue

Illus. 3-136 shows some of the more common joints used for joining two or more pieces of wood.

Labels, Removing

You've just bought a shiny new bench plane and you are ready to use it, but the price sticker you want to remove seems as if it's welded to the base plate. A simple way to remove it is to give it a couple of squirts of WD-40® (Illus. 3-137). Let the WD-40 soak in for a few minutes, and then rub it and the label off with a paper towel.

Laminating
(See Veneers)

Lathe
(Also see Router and Drill Press)

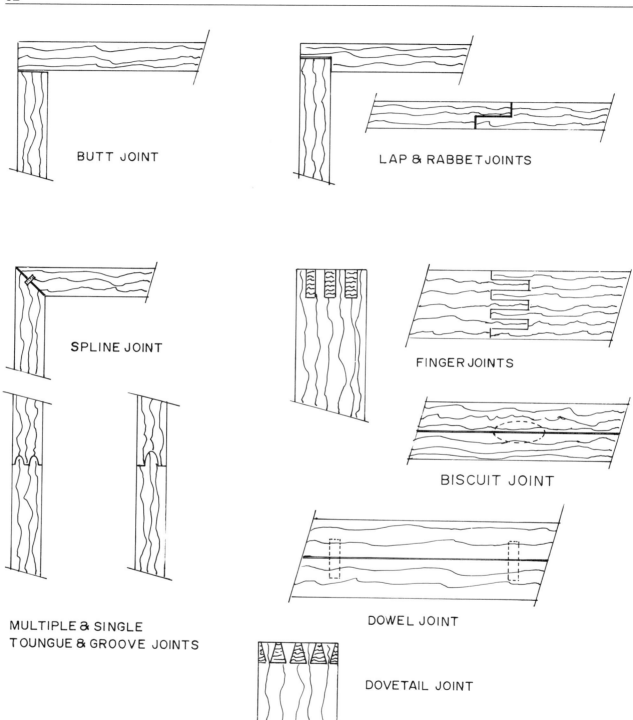

BUTT JOINT

LAP & RABBET JOINTS

SPLINE JOINT

FINGER JOINTS

BISCUIT JOINT

MULTIPLE & SINGLE
TOUNGUE & GROOVE JOINTS

DOWEL JOINT

DOVETAIL JOINT

Illus. 3-136. Common joints.

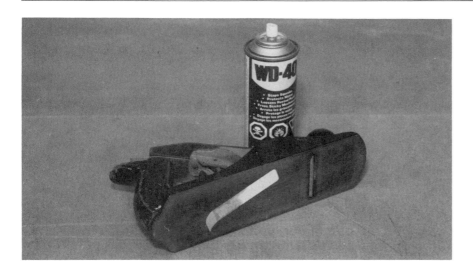

Illus. 3-137. One way to remove a price sticker from a tool is to squirt it with WD-40® and then rub it off with a paper towel.

Lathe Duplicator

Sears sells a Craftsman® copy crafter which can duplicate such things as chair and table legs, etc. (Illus. 3-138). Not only will it copy a turning that you just made, but it will duplicate an existing part as well.

Safety Techniques

Protect yourself from a spinning chuck on your lathe by using an old plastic container (Illus. 3-139). Drill out the bottom and drill a small hole on the side. Now, install the container on the arbor between the motor and the chuck. Adjust it so that the hole on the side of the container gives you access to the chuck screw, if your lathe has one.

Lock Nuts

To prevent nuts and bolts from loosening when they are subject to a lot of vibration, put a drop of "krazy" glue on the bolt just before you tighten it, and then tighten the nut with a wrench. The nut will be tougher to take off, but it shouldn't loosen up by itself.

There is also another product on the market called Threadlocker® (Illus. 3-140) that will prevent nuts and bolts from loosening. It's handy to have around. Try some on your pipe clamps.

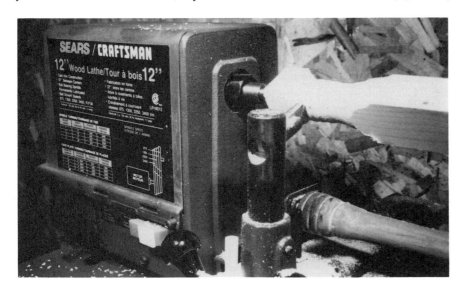

Illus. 3-138. The Sears Lathe Duplicator.

 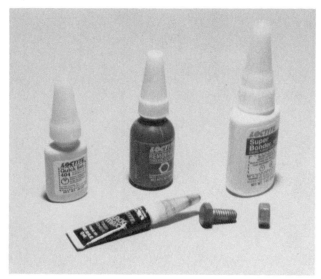

Illus. 3-139 (above left). A safety technique for the lathe. **Illus. 3-140 (above right).** "Krazy" glue or Thread-locker® can be used to prevent nuts and bolts from loosening.

Lubricants

A well-equipped home workshop should have an assortment of lubricants on hand. Chart 3-10 and Illus. 3-141 describe and show various types and brands of lubricants and their uses:

LUBRICANT

WD-40® and LPS 2™
LPS 1™

SILICONE SPRAY

WHITE GREASE AND VASELINE®
3 IN 1 OIL
WAX CANDLE
RUST CHECK

LUBRIPLATE®
Chart 3-10.

Lumber

Definition of Lumber

The term "lumber" as used in this book refers to softwood. Softwood is considered any wood yielded from a coniferous tree.

USES

For loosening rusted nuts and bolts and removing sticky labels.
A light-duty lubricant that forms a sticky film on metals and helps deter corrosion.
Use on sticky drawer rails, machinery tabletops, saw blades, and rubber gaskets.
Use on unsealed bearings, axles, exterior door locks, and hinges.
Use sparingly on motors where indicated, and on hinges and wheels.
Use on drawer rails, window channels, and edges of material to be glued.
Although not a lubricant, it is a rust inhibitor and should be used on machinery tabletops, hand tools, and nuts and bolts.
Use this lubricant on such things as hinges and other slow-moving parts.

Illus. 3-141. Some of the different lubricants available on the market.

Lumber-Buying Guidelines

Most lumberyards sell their product by the board foot, some by the running foot. Determine this beforehand, so you will know how much the lumber will cost. A board foot is a piece of undressed wood that measures 1 inch thick × 12 inches wide × 12 inches long. Chart 3-7 on page 86 is a board-foot chart that will help you determine the quantity of board feet in a piece of dimensioned lumber or hardwood.

Chart 3-11 clarifies the terms used to describe lumber, and wood in general. Charts 3-12 and 3-13 provide information on the grading of lumber.

Never buy lumber over the phone. Select it in person. Choose only straight and true pieces that have no bows, cups, or warps. A bow is a longitudinal bend, a warp is a twist, and a cup is a bend in the width of the piece (Illus. 3-142). Look also for cracks, loose knots, and checks. A check is a crack in the end of the piece.

Home woodworkers have a tendency to buy clear pine for their projects, when, in fact, a *much* less expensive wood will suffice. Clear pine is nearly knot-free. Knotty pine has tight knots and is less expensive. Select spruce has tight knots and is the least expensive of the three. So, if your project is going to be painted, spruce can probably be used.

Lumber may be purchased undressed, dressed on two sides, or dressed on four sides. If you have a thickness planer, buying undressed lumber will save money. Buying lumber dressed on two sides will also save you some money if you are going to put the board on a jointer.

Never buy lumber on the same day that you plan on using it in your workshop. Lumber has to dry, and in doing so will shrink.

Chart 3-14 contains information on appearance lumber, lumber used in all applications where strength is not the primary consideration.

Annual growth ring:	The ring seen on a transverse section of a piece of wood composed of contrasting springwood and summerwood and denoting one year's growth.
Broad-leaved trees:	Trees which shed their leaves in the autumn. Most broad-leaved, or deciduous, trees are hardwoods and have broad leaves.
Cambium:	The one-cell thick layer of tissue between the bark and the wood in a tree. It repeatedly subdivides to form new wood and bark cells.
Cell:	General term for the minute units of wood structure, including wood fibres, vessel segments and other elements.
Cellulose:	The carbohydrate that is the principal constituent of wood. It forms the framework of wood cells.
Characteristics:	Distinguishing features which by their extent, number and character determine the quality of a piece of lumber.
Check:	A lengthwise separation of the wood which usually extends across the rings of annual growth, commonly resulting from stresses set up in wood during seasoning.
Decay:	The decomposition of the wood substance caused by the action of the wood-destroying fungi, resulting in softening, loss of strength and weight, and often in change of texture and colour.
Density:	Weight per unit volume. In the case of wood, density is usually expressed as kilograms per cubic metre at a specified moisture content.
Equilibrium moisture content:	The moisture content at which wood neither gains nor loses moisture when surrounded by air at a given relative humidity and temperature.
Extractives:	Substances in wood (not an integral part of the cellular structure) that can be removed by solution in hot or cold water, benzene, or other solvents that do not react chemically with wood components.
Fibre, wood:	A comparatively long, narrow, tapering wood cell closed at both ends.
Fibre saturation point:	The stage condition of wood in which the cell walls are saturated and the cell cavities are free of water, at approximately 25-30 percent moisture content.
Figure:	The pattern produced in a wood surface by annual growth rings, rays, knots, deviations from regular grain and irregular colouration.
Grain:	The direction, size, arrangement, appearance or quality of the fibre in wood or veneer. To have a specific meaning the term must be qualified.
Cross-grain:	A pattern in which the fibre and other longitudinal elements deviate from a line parallel to the sides of the piece. Applies to either diagonal or spiral grain or a combination of the two.
Diagonal-grain:	Grain in which the longitudinal elements form an angle with the axis of the piece as a result of sawing at an angle with the bark of the tree or log; a form of cross grain.
Edge-grain (rift-sawn, vertical grain, quarter-sawn, quarter cut):	Terms referring to timber or veneer cut in a plane approximately at right angles to the annual rings, and means a condition in which the rings form an angle of 45 degrees or more with the face of the piece.
Flat-grain (flat-sawn, plain-sawn, slash-grain):	Terms referring to timber or veneer cut in a plane approximately tangential to the annual rings, and means a condition in which the rings form an angle of less than 45 degrees with the face of the piece.
Spiral-grain:	An arrangement of the fibres in a piece of timber or veneer which results from their growth in a spiral direction around the bole of the tree.

Chart 3-11 (here and pages 97 and 98). A glossary that defines lumber terms. (Courtesy of Canadian Wood Council)

Straight-grain: A condition where the fibres of the wood run parallel or nearly parallel to the edges of the piece.

Green or unseasoned: Freshly sawed lumber, or lumber that has received no intentional drying. The term does not apply to lumber completely wet because of water-logging.

Hardwoods: Generally one of the botanical groups of trees that have broad leaves in contrast to the conifers or softwoods. The term does not necessarily refer to the actual hardness of the wood.

Heartwood: The inner core of a woody stem wholly composed of nonliving cells and usually differentiated from the outer enveloping layer (sapwood) by its darker colour. It is usually more decay resistant than sapwood.

Knot: That portion of a branch or limb that has been surrounded by subsequent growth of wood of the trunk or other portion of the tree.

Loose knot: A knot which is not held firmly in place by growth or position and which cannot be relied upon to remain in place.

Sound tight knot: A knot so fixed by growth or position that it will retain its place in the piece.

Spike knot: A knot sawn in a lengthwise or nearly lengthwise direction.

Lignin: The second most abundant constituent of wood; the thin cementing layer between the wood cells.

Modulus of rupture: A measure of a beam's ability to support a slowly applied load for a short time. It is an accepted criterion of strength, although it is not a true stress, since the formula by which it is computed is only valid to the proportional limit.

Moisture: Mass of water in wood expressed as a percentage of weight of oven dry wood.

Pitch: Accumulation of resin in wood.

Pitch pocket: An opening between growth rings which usually contains or has contained resin or bark or both.

Pith: The small cylinder of primary tissue of a tree stem around which the annual rings form.

Rays: Strips of cells extending radially within a tree and varying in height from a few cells in some species to 100 mm or more in oak. The rays store food and transport it horizontally in the tree.

Relative density: The ratio of the mass of a body to the mass of an equal volume of water.

Sap: The watery fluid that circulates through a tree carrying the chemical food that enables the tree to grow.

Sapwood: The wood of pale colour near the outside of the log. Under most conditions sapwood is more susceptible to decay than heartwood.

Seasoning: The process of drying timber to a moisture content appropriate for the conditions and purposes for which it is to be used.

Air-dried: Dried by exposure to air, usually in a yard, without artificial heat.

Kiln-dried: Dried in a kiln with the use of artificial heat.

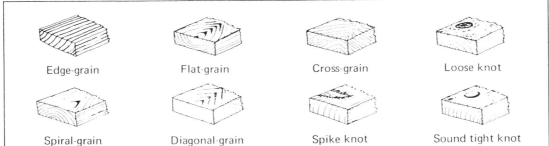

Edge-grain Flat-grain Cross-grain Loose knot

Spiral-grain Diagonal-grain Spike knot Sound tight knot

Chart 3-11 continued.

Shake:	A separation along the grain, the greater part of which occurs between the rings of annual growth.	Texture:	The relative size and arrangement of the wood cells.
Shrinkage:	The decrease in the dimensions of wood owing to a decrease of moisture content.	Vessels: (hardwoods only)	Wood cells of comparatively large diameter that have open ends and are set one above the other so as to form continuous tubes. The openings of the vessels on the surface of a piece of wood are usually referred to as pores.
Slope of grain:	The angle between the direction of the grain and the axis of the piece, expressed as a slope and measured over a distance which will assure the determination of the general slope of the grain, not influenced by short local deviations.	Wane:	The bark or lack of wood from any cause on the face of a piece.
		Warp:	Any deviation from a true or plane surface. Warp includes bow, crook, cup and twist, and any combination thereof.
Softwoods:	Generally, one of the botanical groups of trees that in most cases have needlelike or scalelike leaves, the conifers. The term does not refer to the actual hardness of the wood.	Bow:	A deviation flatwise from a straight line (a curve along the face of the piece) from end to end of a piece, measured at the point of greatest deviation.
Species:	A distinct sort or kind of tree. A class of trees having some characteristics or qualities in common that distinguish them from other similar groups.	Crook:	The deviation of the edges of a piece from a straight line drawn from end to end of the piece, and is measured at the point of greatest distance from the straight line.
Split:	A separation along the grain, forming a crack or fissure that extends through the piece from one surface to another.	Cup:	A deviation flatwise from a straight line (a curve across the face of a piece) across the width of a piece measured at the point of greatest deviation.
Springwood:	The portion of the annual growth ring that is formed during the early part of the season's growth; it is usually less dense, lighter in colour, and weaker mechanically than summerwood.	Twist:	Warping in which one corner of a piece twists out of the plane of the other three; amount of twist is determined by measuring the normal distance of one corner of the piece from the plane of the other three.
Stain:	A discolouration on or in lumber other than its natural colour.		
Summerwood:	The portion of the annual growth that is formed after the springwood formation has ceased. It is usually more dense and stronger mechanically than springwood.	Wood substance:	The solid material of which wood is composed.

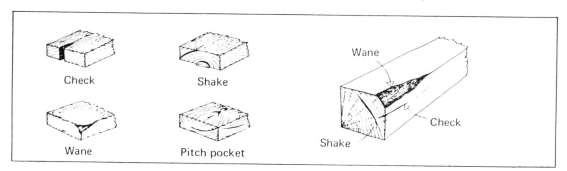

Check   Shake

Wane   Pitch pocket

Wane   Check   Shake

Chart 3-11 continued.

Integrity of Grade Stamp

Western Wood Products Association is the largest association of lumber manufacturers in the United States. WWPA members and grading service subscribers are located in the 12 western states: Arizona, California, Colorado, Idaho, Montana, Nevada, New Mexico, Oregon, South Dakota, Utah, Washington and Wyoming. The Association's Quality Standards Department supervises lumber grading by maintaining a highly competent staff of lumber inspectors who regularly check the quality of mill production, including visual grade requirements of glued products and machine stress-rated lumber.

The Association's *Grading Rules for Western Lumber* establishes standards of size and levels of quality in conformance with the American Softwood Lumber Standard PS 20-70. The Association is certified as a rules writing and inspection agency by the Board of Review, American Lumber Standards Committee. The Association is approved to provide mill supervisory services under its rules and the rules of the West Coast Lumber Inspection Bureau, the National Lumber Grades Authority for Canadian Lumber and the NGR portion of the Southern Pine Inspection Bureau Rules. In addition, WWPA is approved to supervise finger-jointed and machine stress-rated lumber. Under the rules of the Redwood Inspection Service, the Association is approved for studs.

Interpreting Grade Marks

Most grade stamps, except those for rough lumber or heavy timbers, contain 5 basic elements:

a. WWPA certification mark. Certifies Association quality supervision. ⓦ⊚ is a registered trademark.

b. Mill identification. Firm name, brand or assigned mill number. WWPA can be contacted to identify an individual mill whenever necessary.

c. Grade designation. Grade name, number or abbreviation.

d. Species identification. Indicates species by individual species or species combination. New* species identification marks for groups to which design values are assigned are:

e. Condition of seasoning. Indicates condition of seasoning at time of surfacing:

MC-15 — 15% maximum moisture content
S-DRY — 19% maximum moisture content
S-GRN — over 19% moisture content (unseasoned)

*Effective upon publication of *Western Lumber Grading Rules '91*, September 15, 1991.

Inspection Certificate

When an inspection certificate issued by the Western Wood Products Association is required on a shipment of lumber and specific grade marks are not used, the stock is identified by an imprint of the Association mark and the number of the shipping mill or inspector.

Grade Stamp Facsimiles

WWPA uses a set of marks similar to the randomly selected examples shown on the reverse side, to identify lumber graded under its supervision.

Species Combinations

The species groupings for dimension lumber products are shown left and explained in the second box on the reverse side. When alternative species combinations, as shown in the third box on the reverse side, are used for structural applications, design values are controlled by the species with the lowest strength value within the combination.

Chart 3-12 (here and pages 100–104). Chart detailing the grading system of American lumber. (Courtesy of Western Wood Products)

The facsimile grade stamps and grading agency information presented here is published as an industry service with the permission of ALSC.

May, 1992
(supersedes all previous lists)

Accredited Agencies and Typical Grade Stamps as approved by the Board of Review of the American Lumber Standards Committee.

American Lumber Standards Committee
P.O. Box 210
Germantown, Maryland 20875-0210
TELE: 301/972-1700
FAX: 301/540-8004

TYPICAL GRADE STAMPS

ACCREDITED AGENCIES NAMES AND ADDRESSES

California Lumber Inspection Service
1885 The Alameda
Box 6989
San Jose, California 95150
408/241-2960
FAX: 408/246-5415

Approval as an inspection agency including mill supervisory service under the WCLIB rules, the WWPA rules, RIS rules, the National Grading Rule (NGR) portion of the NLGA rules for Canadian lumber, and for Boards, Scaffold Plank, and the NGR portion of the SPIB rules. Approved to supervise fingerjointing.

Northeastern Lumber Manufacturers Association, Inc.
272 Tuttle Road, P.O. Box 87A
Cumberland Center, Maine 04021
207/829-6901
FAX: 207/829-4293

Approval of rules they publish and as an inspection agency including mill supervisory service under these rules, the NSLB rules, the NGR portions of the WCLIB rules, the WWPA rules and NLGA rules for Canadian lumber, for Selects and Common Boards, 4/4 Shop, Heavy Shop, for Posts and Timbers, and Beams and Stringers under the WWPA rules, for Posts and Timbers, and Beams and Stringers under the WCLIB rules. NELMA is a rules-writing agency.

Chart 3-12 continued.

110 STUD
S-DRY
BALSAM
FIR

110 STUD
S-DRY
BALSAM
FIR

Northern Softwood Lumber Bureau
(Formerly Northern Hardwood and Pine Manufacturers Association, Inc.)
272 Tuttle Road, P.O. Box 87A
Cumberland Center, Maine 04021
207/829-6901
FAX: 207/829-4293

Approval of rules they publish and as an inspection agency including mill supervisory service under these rules and the NGR portions of the WCLIB rules, the WWPA rules, and the NLGA rules for Canadian lumber. Approved to supervise fingerjointing. NSLB is a rules-writing agency.

PLIB®
W-10
CONST
S-GRN
HEM-FIR   WCLB RULES

Pacific Lumber Inspection Bureau, Inc.
P.O. Box 7235
Bellevue, Washington 98008-1235
206/746-6542
FAX: 206/746-5522

Approval as an inspection agency including mill supervisory service under the WCLIB rules, the WWPA rules, the RIS rules and the NLGA rules for Canadian lumber. Approved to supervise machine stress-rated lumber.

(50) FDTN
S-GRN
REDWOOD **R∤S.**

Redwood Inspection Service
405 Enfrente Drive, Suite 200
Novato, California 94949
415/382-0662
FAX: 415/382-8531

Approval of rules they publish and as an inspection agency including mill supervisory service under these rules, the WCLIB rules, and the WWPA rules. RIS is a rules-writing agency.

SPIB®   No. 1
KD 15   (7)

Southern Pine Inspection Bureau
4709 Scenic Highway
Pensacola, Florida 32504
904/434-2611
FAX: 904/433-5594

Approval of the rules they publish and as an inspection agency including mill supervisory service under these rules and the NGR portions of the NELMA rules, the WWPA rules, the WCLIB rules, and the NLGA rules for Canadian lumber. Approved to supervise fingerjointing and machine stress-rated lumber. SPIB is a rules-writing agency.

TP® NO.1 KD-19
000 S-DRY **SYP**

TP® No 1
S-DRY
000 D.FIR   WWPA Rules

Timber Products Inspection
P.O. Box 919
Conyers, Georgia 30207
404/922-8000
FAX: 404/922-1290

Approval as an inspection agency including mill supervisory service under the RIS rules, the SPIB rules, the WCLIB rules, the WWPA rules and the NGR portions of the NELMA rules, the NLGA rules for Canadian lumber and the NSLB rules, and for Posts and Timbers, and Beams and Stringers under the NELMA rules. Approved to supervise fingerjointing and machine stress-rated lumber.

Chart 3-12 continued.

MILL 10
NO. 2
DOUG FIR   S-DRY

West Coast Lumber Inspection Bureau
Box 23145
Portland, Oregon 97223
503/639-0651
FAX: 503/684-8928

Approval of rules they publish and as an inspection agency including mill supervisory service under these rules, the RIS rules, the WWPA rules, the NLGA rules for Canadian lumber, the Scaffold, Boards, Radius Edge Decking, Finish and NGR portions under the SPIB rules. Approved to supervise fingerjointing and machine stress-rated lumber. WCLIB is a rules-writing agency.

12
Ⓦ. **2**   S-DRY   /D.\FIR\

Western Wood Products Association
Yeon Building
522 SW Fifth Avenue
Portland, Oregon 97204-2122
503/224-3930
FAX: 503/224-3934

Approval of rules they publish and as an inspection agency including mill supervisory service under these rules, the WCLIB rules, the NLGA rules for Canadian lumber, for Studs under the RIS rules, and the Scaffold and the NGR portion of the SPIB rules. Approved to supervise fingerjointing and machine stress-rated lumber. WWPA is a rules-writing agency.

CANADIAN STAMPS

The following Canadian agencies have been accredited by the Board of Review of the American Lumber Standards Committee as inspection agencies including mill supervisory service under the National Lumber Grades Authority (NLGA) for Canadian Lumber. The NLGA is the rules-writing agency for Canada.

**National Lumber
Grades Authority**
260-1055 West Hastings Street
Vancouver, BC V6E 2E9
604/689-1563
FAX: 604/687-8036

**ACCREDITED AGENCIES
NAMES AND ADDRESSES**

A.F.P.A.® 00
S — P — F
S-DRY STAND

C L® A
S-P-F
100
No. 2
S-GRN.

C L® A 100
SPRUCE PINE FIR
NO. 1   S-DRY

Ⓛ MA 0 S-DRY 1
0 S—P—F

CFPA® 00
S-P-F S-DRY
CONST

**Alberta Forest Products
Association**
11710 Kingsway Avenue, #104
Edmonton, Alberta T5G 0X5
403/452-2841   FAX: 403/455-0505
Approved to supervise fingerjointing and machine stress-rated lumber.

**Canadian Lumbermen's
Association**
27 Goulburn Avenue
Ottawa, Ontario K1N 8C7
613/233-6205   FAX: 613/233-1929
Approved to provide supervisory service under NGR portion of the NELMA rules.

**Cariboo Lumber Manufacturers
Association**
304-172 N. 2nd Avenue
Williams Lake, B.C. V2G 1Z6
604/392-7778   FAX: 604/392-4692
Approved to supervise fingerjointing and machine stress-rated lumber.

**Central Forest Products
Association, Inc.**
P.O. Box 1169
Hudson Bay, Saskatchewan S0E 0Y0
306/865-2595   FAX: 306/865-3302

Chart 3-12 continued.

CQA® 100   S-P-F S-GRN No 1

ILMA® 00   S-DRY 1   S—P—F

0 **(M)** 0   No 1 S-DRY D FIR (N)

M L B | S-P-F NO. 1 S-GRN 85

O.L.M.A.® 01-1
CONST.   S-DRY
SPRUCE - PINE - FIR

QLB®   00   NLGA RULE No 1 S-GRN HEM-FIR-N

®S P F 03 1 S-GRN

Council of Forest Industries of British Columbia
1200-555 Burrard Street
Vancouver, B.C. V7X 1S7
604/684-0211   FAX: 604/687-4930
Approved to supervise fingerjointing and machine stress-rated lumber.

Interior Lumber Manufacturers Association
360-1855 Kirschner Road
Kelowna, B.C. V1Y 4N7
604/860-9663   FAX: 604/860-0009
Approved to supervise fingerjointing and machine stress-rated lumber.

MacDonald Inspection
211 Schoolhouse Street
Coquitlam, B.C. V3K 4X9
604/520-3321   FAX:604/524-9186
Approved to supervise fingerjointing and machine stress-rated lumber.

Maritime Lumber Bureau
P.O. Box 459
Amherst, Nova Scotia B4H 4A1
902/667-3880   FAX: 902/667-0401
Approved to provide supervisory service under the NGR portion of the NELMA rules.

Ontario Lumber Manufacturers Association
55 University Avenue, Suite 325
Box 8
Toronto, Ontario M5J 2H7
416/367-9717   FAX: 416/862-2498
Approved to supervise machine stress-rated lumber. Also, approved to provide supervisory service under the NGR portion of the NELMA rules.

Pacific Lumber Inspection Bureau
P.O. Box 7235
Bellevue, Washington 98008-1235
B.C. Division:
1110-355 Burrard Street
Vancouver, B.C. V6C 2G8
604/689-1561   FAX: 604/689-0292
Approved to supervise machine stress-rated lumber.

Quebec Lumber Manufacturers Association
5055 West Hamel Blvd., Suite 200
Quebec, QB G2E 2G6
418/872-5610   FAX:418/872-3062
Approved to supervise fingerjointing. Also, approved to provide supervisory service under the NGR portion of the NELMA rules.

American Lumber Standards Committee
W.F. Hammond, Chairman
R.B. Parrish, Vice Chairman
B.W. Ingram, Treasurer
T.D. Searles, Executive
   Vice President

Additional information about approved grade stamps and agencies is available from:

American Lumber Standards Committee
P.O. Box 210
Germantown, MD 20875-0210
301/972-1700
FAX: 301/540-8004

Chart 3-12 continued.

Facsimiles of Typical Grade Stamps

Perpetuating America's Forests for Products and the Environment.

Dimension Grades

Glued Products

Finish Grade — Graded Under WCLIB Rules

Cedar Grades

Commons

Machine Stress-Rated Products

MACHINE RATED

1650 Fb 1.5E

MACHINE RATED

1650Fb 1020Ft 1.5E

Finish & Select Grades

Decking

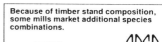

Species Identification

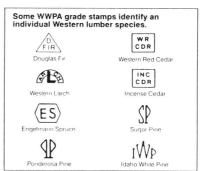

Chart 3-12 continued.

A.F.P.A. 00
S—P—F
S-DRY STAND

Alberta Forest Products
  Association
11710 Kingsway Avenue
Suite 204
Edmonton, Alta. T5G 0X5

M L B | SPRUCE PINE FIR **STAND** S-GRN
MILL 11 — 466

Maritime Lumber Bureau
P.O. Box 459
Amherst, N.S. B4H 4A1

C L A
S-P-F
100
No. 2
S-GRN.

Canadian Lumbermen's
  Association
27 Goulburn Avenue
Ottawa, Ont. K1N 8C7

O.L.M.A. 01-1
CONST. S-DRY
SPRUCE - PINE - FIR

Ontario Lumber Manufacturers
  Association
55 York Street
Suite 1312
Toronto, Ont. M5J 1R7

(LMA) 1 S-GRN 1
      1 D FIR (N)

Cariboo Lumber Manufacturers
  Association
197 Second Avenue North
Suite 301
Williams Lake, B.C. V2G 1Z5

STUD
031

Quebec Lumber Manufacturers
  Association
3555 Boulevard Hamel W.
Suite 200
Quebec, P.Q. G2E 2G6

CFPA 00
S·P·F S DRY
CONST

Central Forest Products
  Association
P.O. Box 1169
Hudson Bay, Sask. S0E 0Y0

0 (M) No 1
       S-DRY
0   D FIR (N)
    NLGA RULE

MacDonald Inspection
211 School House Street
Coquitlam, B.C. V3K 4X9

 **S-P-F**
S-DRY
100 **No 2**

Council of Forest Industries
  of British Columbia
1055 West Hastings Street
Suite 1500
Vancouver, B.C. V6E 2H1
          and
Council of Forest Industries
  of British Columbia
Northern Interior Lumber Sector
299 Victoria Street,
Suite 803
Prince George, B.C. V2L 2J5

Nwt 10
CONST S-P-F
     S-GRN

N.W.T. Grade Stamping
  Agency
P.O. Box 1302
Yellowknife, N.W.T. X0E 1J7

ILMA S-DRY **1**
0 0 S—P—F

Interior Lumber Manufacturers
  Association
2350 Hunter Road
Suite 203
Kelowna, B.C. V1X 6C1

PLIB **NLGA RULE**
      No 1
      S-GRN
0 0 **HEM-FIR-N**

Pacific Lumber Inspection
  Bureau
1055 West Hastings Street
Suite 1460
Vancouver, B.C. V6E 2G8

Chart 3-13 (here and page 106). Chart detailing the grades and uses of lumber. (Courtesy of Canadian Wood Council)

TABLE 2   Dimension Lumber — Grades and Uses

Sizes (mm)	Grades	Common Grade mix [1]	Principal uses	Grade Category
38 to 89 mm thick, 38 to 89 mm wide	Select structural No. 1 No. 2	No. 2 and Better (No. 2 & Btr.)	Most common; used in most construction. Shows high strength, stiffness and good appearance. Preferred for trusses, rafters and roof joists.	Structural Light Framing
	No. 3 [3]		Used in construction where high strength and appearance are not important, such as Studs in non-load bearing walls.	Light Framing
	Construction [3] Standard [3]	Standard and Better (Std. & Btr.)	Most common; used in general framing work. Has less strength and smaller spans than No. 2 & Btr. structural light framing, but is stronger and allows longer spans than No. 3.	
	Utility [2]	—	Used most economically where high strength is not important, such as studs and plates in partition walls, blocking and bracing.	
	Economy [2]	—	Used in temporary or low cost construction where strength and appearance are not important.	
38 to 89 mm thick, 114 mm and wider	Select structural No. 1 No. 2	No. 2 & Btr.	Most common; used in most construction where high strength and stiffness are desired, such as floor joists, roof joists and rafters.	Structural Joists and Planks
	No. 3 [3]	—	Used in general construction where strength is not important.	
	Economy [2]	—	Used in temporary or low cost construction where strength and appearance are not important.	
38 × 38, 38 × 64, 38 × 89, 38 × 140, 64 × 64, 64 × 89, 89 × 89	Stud [3]	—	Most common; special purpose grade intended for all stud uses.	Stud
	Economy Stud [2]	—	Used in temporary or low cost construction where strength and appearance are not important.	

Notes: (1) For ease in grade sorting at the mill, the higher grades are combined and sold as a grade mix. Pieces of lumber in the grade mix are still individually grade stamped.

(2) Except for the utility and economy grades, all grades are stress graded which means specified strengths have been assigned and span tables calculated. Specified strengths for the commercial softwood species are given in CWC datafile WD-2, *Lumber Design.*

(3) Construction, Standard, Stud and No. 3 Grades should not be used in designs that are not composed of 3 or more essentially parallel members spaced on 610 mm centres or less, so arranged or connected to mutually support loading.

Chart 3-13 continued.

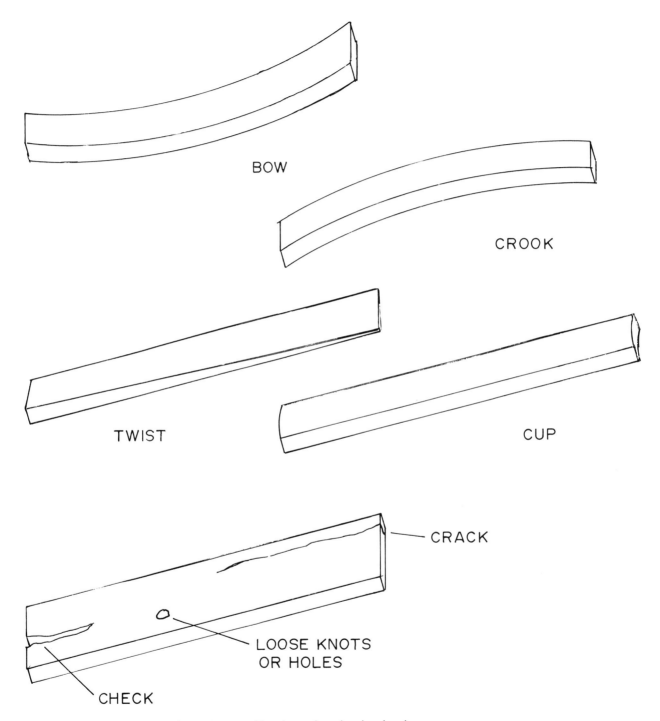

BOW

CROOK

TWIST

CUP

CRACK

LOOSE KNOTS
OR HOLES

CHECK

Illus. 3-142. Do not choose these types of lumber when buying lumber.

INTRODUCTION

The lumber grades in this category are intended for applications where strength is not the primary consideration. Grading is by visual inspection and is a judgment of appearance and suitability to end use rather than of strength. Natural characteristics and manufacturing imperfections are taken into account in the assigning of grades. Lumber in this category is often generically referred to as Board Lumber, although the category also includes run-to-pattern products and Patio Decking. The highest grades of Appearance Lumber are seldom gradestamped, unless on the back or ends, as the grade stamp would deface the product. The general purpose grades, such as COMMONS and ALTERNATE BOARDS, are generally stamped. Refer to page 20 for additional information on grade stamps, moisture content and specifying Appearance Lumber.

Many of the Western Lumber species are grown, harvested, manufactured and shipped together in "Marketing Categories". In addition to the species combinations that share like structural characteristics, Board Lumber is often available in combinations related to like appearance characteristics. Refer to the Marketing Categories species list on page 4 and the WWPA *Western Lumber Grading Rules* for additional information.

The grades and recommended end uses for Appearance Lumber are explained in Table 14. Standard sizes are explained in Table 15. Refer to page 19 for information on the Radius-edged Patio Decking grades.

APPEARANCE LUMBER GRADES — Table 14

	Product	Grades*	Equivalent Grades in Idaho White Pine	WWPA Grading Rules Section Number
Highest Quality Appearance Grades	SELECTS *(all species)*	B & Btr Select	Supreme	10.11
		C Select	Choice	10.12
		D Select	Quality	10.13
	FINISH *(usually available only in Doug Fir and Hem-Fir)*	Superior		10.51
		Prime		10.52
		E		10.53
	SPECIAL WESTERN RED CEDAR PATTERN GRADES	Clear Heart		20.11
		A Grade		20.12
		B Grade		20.13
General Purpose Grades	COMMON BOARDS (WWPA Rules) *(primarily in pines, spruces and cedars)*	1 Common	Colonial	30.11
		2 Common	Sterling	30.12
		3 Common	Standard	30.13
		4 Common	Utility	30.14
		5 Common	Industrial	30.15
	ALTERNATE BOARDS (WCLIB Rules) *(primarily in Doug Fir and Hem-Fir)*			**WCLIB**
		Select Merchantable		118-a
		Construction		118-b
		Standard		118-c
		Utility		118-d
		Economy		118-e
	SPECIAL WESTERN RED CEDAR PATTERN GRADES			**WCLIB**
		Select Knotty		111-e
		Quality Knotty		111-f

*Refer to WWPA's, *Vol. 2. Western Wood Species* book for full-color photographs.

BOARD LUMBER

Grades/End Uses - Select grades are determined from the better side or face and are used for applications where only the finest appearance is appropriate. B & BTR is virtually clear, and very limited in availability. C and D SELECTS are only slightly less perfect.

Finish grades are determined from the better side or face and from both edges on pieces 5″ and narrower and from the better side or face and edge on pieces 6″ and wider. SUPERIOR is virtually clear. PRIME grade exhibits fine appearance although slightly less restrictive than SUPERIOR. E grade is intended for ripping and cross-cutting to obtain small pieces of PRIME or better quality.

Cedar CLEAR grades are typically run-to-pattern into siding or paneling products and may be graded to either the surfaced or a saw-textured side. CLEAR VG HEART is intended for use where only the highest quality is indicated. The exposed width is all heartwood and free from imperfections. A grade allows only minor imperfections and is of fine appearance. Square-edged cedar boards are generally manufactured in SELECT grades.

Common Board grades are determined from the better face and are varying qualities of knotty material. 1 and 2 COMMON are usually sold as 2 & BTR COMMON and intended for paneling, shelving and other uses where a fine appearance in knotty material is desirable. 3 COMMON is also widely used for siding, paneling and shelving as well as for fences, boxes, crating, sheathing and industrial applications. 4 COMMON is more widely used than any other grade for general construction such as subfloors, roof & wall sheathing, concrete forms, low-cost fencing, crating, etc. 5 COMMON is intended for economy-governed applications.

Alternate Board grades are determined from the better face. SELECT MERCHANTABLE is intended for use in housing and light construction where it is exposed as paneling, shelving and where knotty type lumber of fine appearance is desirable. CONSTRUCTION is used for spaced sheathing, let-in bracing, fences, boxes, crating and industrial applications. The uses for STANDARD are similar to a 4 COMMON, as described above.

Special Western Red Cedar general purpose grades (SELECT KNOTTY or QUALITY KNOTTY) are similar in appearance to 2 COMMON and 3 COMMON, and are widely used for siding and landscape applications. Knot size and quality are defined in the grading rules; sound, tight knots do not adversely affect performance. Dry knotty siding must not exceed 19% moisture content, however it may be specified to MC-15. Knotty siding is also sometimes manufactured unseasoned.

RUN-TO-PATTERN PRODUCTS

Board Lumber is the starting material for many products that are run-to-pattern, such as paneling, siding, flooring, ceiling and partition material. In many cases, the grade of the material that has been run-to-pattern reflects the grade of the starting material, adhering to similar requirements for allowable characteristics.

Chart 3-14 (here and pages 109 and 110). Information on the grading of appearance lumber, lumber used in application where strength is not the primary consideration. (Courtesy of WWPA)

SPECIFYING FINISH CARPENTRY MATERIALS

A specification for a Finish or Board Lumber grade should include a reference to the section number, title and edition of the grading rules from which it is written. In other words, if you are specifying from Section 21.11, special Western Red Cedar Rules, WWPA *Western Lumber Grading Rules '91*, so state.

Grain patterns, when desired, can also be specified for Selects, Finish and Special Western Red Cedar grades. Three categories are available: vertical grain (VG), flat grain (FG) or a shipment of both VG and FG, generally referred to as mixed grain (MG). The most readily available and least costly is mixed grain. Unless otherwise specified, siding, paneling and finish boards are shipped with mixed grain. Stair treads, stepping, etc. should be vertical grain as it is more durable.

Board Lumber in Combination with Rough Carpentry Materials - Boards, basically, are 1″ nominal thickness. Board grades used in conjunction with rough carpentry materials are generally controlled by building code requirements, and the grades are selected from the Common or Alternate Board grades listed in the appearance lumber grades chart on page 18, Table 14.

As an example, major model building codes recognize NO. 3 COMMON or STANDARD grades as equal minimum grades for spaced roof sheathing even though there are differences in grading characteristics. Verify local building code requirements and dealer availability prior to specifying.

Seasoning Appearance Lumber - Once in place, lumber adjusts to its surrounding atmospheric conditions. In a covered structure, lumber will stabilize at approximately 6 to 12% moisture content. Size will vary approximately 1% for each 4% change in moisture content. Thus, it is important that all finish materials be stacked and stickered, in the room where they will be applied for 7-10 days prior to installation. The lumber should be stored off the ground, well ventilated and loosely covered. The lumber will then stabilize its moisture content for its permanent location. Staining or priming, where economically feasible, should be done before installation. Refer to WWPA *Paneling Basics* (A-3), *Natural Wood Siding* (TG-8) and *Lumber Storage* (TG-5) for additional information.

Moisture Content - WWPA Finish and Select grades, as well as special Western Red Cedar grades, are shipped seasoned as follows: *S-DRY or MC-15 with at least 85 percent of items not exceeding 12% in moisture content and no portion exceeding 15% moisture content.* Appearance grades of Western Lumber are not shipped S-GRN (with a moisture content above 19% at the time of surfacing) except in some of the knotty grades. Refer to page 4 for additional information on moisture content designations in the grade stamp and to WWPA's *Natural Wood Siding* (TG-8) for recommendations on handling unseasoned siding products.

Chart 3-14 continued.

Interior and Exterior Trim and Finish Board Materials
Select from appearance grades as indicated in Table 14 and described in the WWPA *Western Lumber Grading Rules '91*.

Refer to the WWPA publication, *Vol. 2: Western Wood Species* for color photographs of Select, Finish, Common and Alternate Board grades in many Western Lumber species.

Wood Siding and Paneling Materials - The following publications offer information on selecting pattern type and grade, and summarize installation and handling requirements: *Natural Wood Siding: A Technical Guide* (TG-8), *Siding Basics, A Field Guide* (A-8) and *Paneling Basics* (A-3).

After a general pattern type has been selected, the pattern number should be specified from the WWPA publication *Standard Patterns* (G-16).

When a saw-textured face is desired, the face to be textured and the type of texture (band sawn, rough sawn, circular sawn, etc.) should be specified.

A siding specification should include WWPA's industry recommendations for acclimatization, backpriming, nailing and finishing. Refer to WWPA's *Natural Wood Siding* (TG-8) for details. A checklist and moisture content guidelines are provided below for convenience.

MOISTURE CONTENT GUIDELINES

Uses of Wood	Recommended Moisture Content at Time of Installation					
	Most Areas of the U.S		Dry, Southwestern States		Damp, Warm Southeastern Coastal Areas	
	Average[1]	Individual Pieces	Average[1]	Individual Pieces	Average[1]	Individual Pieces
Siding, Trim and Sheathing	12%	9-14%	9%	7-12%	12%	9-14%

[1] To obtain a realistic average, test at least 10% of each item, i.e. 10% of the siding pieces, 10% of the trim pieces and random checks of the sheathing material. It is particularly important to check the sheathing prior to the siding application if it has become wet after it was installed.

Source: Wood Handbook, 1987, from Table 14-1.

SIDING OR PANELING MATERIAL SPECIFICATION
Checklist 5

☐ Select species suited to the project.
☐ List grade names, paragraph numbers and rules-writing agency. *(Refer to Table 14)*
☐ Specify surface texture for exposed face.
☐ Specify moisture content suited to project.
☐ If gradestamped, specify lumber be stamped on back or ends. (WWPA's *Lumber Specifying* offers additional information.)
☐ Specify VG (vertical grain) if appropriate and available.
☐ Specify pattern and size. (WWPA's *Standard Patterns* offers additional information.)
☐ Specify installation, nailing and finishing. (WWPA's *Natural Wood Siding* offers additional information.)

STANDARD SIZES-APPEARANCE LUMBER

Table 15

Nominal & Dressed
Based on *Western Lumber Grading Rules*

Product	Description	Nominal Size		Dry Dressed Dimensions		
		Thickness (inches)	Width (inches)	Thickness (inches)	Width (inches)	Lengths (feet)
SELECTS AND COMMONS	S1S, S2S, S4S, S1S1E, S1S2E	4/4	2	¾	1 ½	6' and longer
		5/4	3	1 5/32	2 ½	in multiples
		6/4	4	1 13/32	3 ½	of 1' except
		7/4	5	1 19/32	4 ½	Douglas Fir
		8/4	6	1 13/16	5 ½	and Larch
		9/4	7	2 3/32	6 ½	Selects shall be
		10/4	8 & wider	2 3/8	¾ off	4' and longer
		11/4		2 9/16	nominal	with 3% of 4'
		12/4		2 ¾		and 5'
		16/4		3 ¾		permitted.
FINISH AND ALTERNATE BOARD GRADES	S1S, S2S, S4S, S1S1E, S1S2E	⅜	2	5/16	1 ½	3' and longer.
		½	3	7/16	2 ½	In Superior
		⅝	4	9/16	3 ½	grade, 3% of 3'
		¾	5	⅝	4 ½	and 4' and 7%
	(Only these sizes apply to Alternate Board Grades.)	1	6	¾	5 ½	of 5' and 6'
		1 ¼	7	1	6 ½	are permitted.
		1 ½	8 & wider	1 ¼	¾ off	In Prime Grade
		1 ¾		1 ⅜	nominal	20% of 3' to 6'
		2		1 ½		is permitted.
		2 ½		2		
		3		2 ½		
		3 ½		3		
		4		3 ½		

Abbreviations:
S1S - Surfaced one side
S2S - Surfaced two sides
S4S - Surfaced four sides
S1S1E - Surfaced one side, one edge.
S1S2E - Surfaced one side, two edges.

Chart 3-14 continued.

Nominal and Dressed Sizes of Lumber

Chart 3-15 shows the rough size and the actual dressed size for different sizes of lumber.

Nominal (Rough Size)	Actual Dressed Size
1 × 4 inches	¾ × 3½ inches
2 × 2 inches	1½ × 1½ inches
2 × 4 inches	1½ × 3½ inches
2 × 6 inches	1½ × 5½ inches
1 × 6 inches	¾ × 5½ inches

Chart 3-15. The nominal and actual dressed sizes of lumber. (Chart courtesy of Forest Industries of British Columbia)

Softwood Lumber

Chart 3-16 lists some of the softwood species of lumber.

Storing Lumber

If you are storing your pieces of lumber on top of each other on a rack where only the ends or the edges of the lumber are visible, it is usually difficult to determine what kind of wood it is (e.g., pine, spruce, walnut) and how long it is.

Here is a simple solution: First, use colored plastic tape to identify the type of wood. For example, use yellow plastic tape for oak, blue for pine, etc. (Illus. 3-143). Your local hardware store sells plastic tape in packages of five or six colors.

Second, to determine the length of each piece, write its length on the end of the board with a dark pencil or a felt marker (Illus. 3-144). If you end up cutting a piece off a board, write in the new length.

Softwood Species of Lumber

Cedar (Alaska, Atlantic white, eastern red, incense, northern white, Port-Orforde, and western red)

Douglas Fir (coastal, interior north, and interior west)

Fir (balsam, California red, grand, noble, Pacific silver, subalpine, and white)

Hemlock (eastern, mountain, western, shortleaf, slash, sugar, Virginia, and western white)

Larch (western)

Pine (eastern white, jack, loblolly, lodgepole, longleaf, pitch, pond, ponderosa, red, shortleaf, slash, sugar, Virginia, and western)

Spruce (black, Englemann, red, and Sitka)

Tamarack

Chart 3-16.

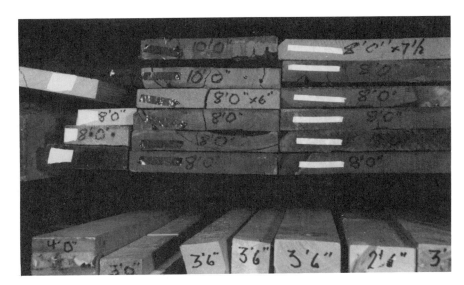

Illus. 3-143. Colored plastic tape can be used to identify different types of wood.

Illus. 3-144. Write the length of a board on its end with a dark pencil or felt-tip pencil.

Magnets

Half-inch-diameter, button-type magnets can prove to be indispensable around the workshop. Stick one to the top of your drill press cover to attach the chuck key to. Attach one to your router table for the wrench (Illus. 3-145). They will even hold a mitre gauge firmly to a table saw or a band saw.

Illus. 3-145. This wrench is attached to the router table with a magnet.

Illus. 3-146. The magnet attached to the end of this broom handle is being used to pick up nails.

Another way to use magnets is to attach one (any type will do) to the end of a broom handle with epoxy glue. You can use this magnet to pick up those small screws, finishing nails, and staples that drop on the floor (Illus. 3-146). Next time you visit your local hardware store, pick up a dozen or so of these magnets. They only cost about 25 cents each.

Masonite

(See Hardboard)

Measuring Technique

It happens to all of us more often than we would care to remember. You want something cut at 41 inches, but you measure and mark 31 inches, and end up with a piece 10 inches too short. Of course, this is your last piece, so it's off to the lumberyard.

Here is an old rule worth mentioning: Measure twice, cut once (Illus. 3-147).

Mitre Gauge

Gripping a Workpiece

Your mitre gauge will better grip the workpiece if you adhere a piece of emery cloth or sandpaper to the face of the gauge with double-faced tape (Illus. 3-148). It will prevent your workpiece from slipping while you are cutting or routing.

Squaring a Mitre Gauge

The screw-down pointer on your mitre gauge can sometimes be knocked out of alignment if you happen to drop

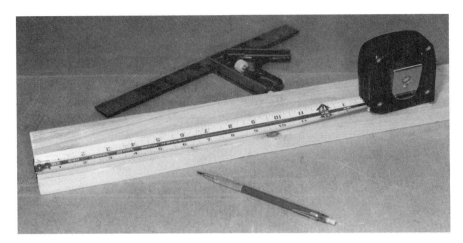

Illus. 3-147. Always measure a piece twice before cutting it.

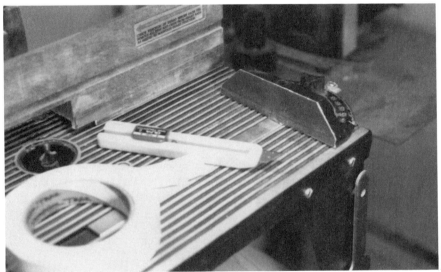

Illus. 3-148. To prevent your workpiece from slipping when you are cutting or routing, adhere a piece of sandpaper to the face of the mitre gauge with double-faced tape.

Illus. 3-149. To determine that the mitre gauge is accurately aligned, turn it upside down, loosen the adjusting knob, slide it into the groove on the tool table, and press it against the table edge.

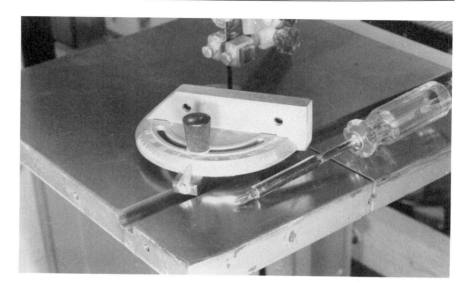

Illus. 3-150. Tighten the knob on the mitre gauge and adjust the pointer if necessary.

or hit the gauge. To ensure a true mitre every time, check the accuracy of the mitre gauge occasionally.

The easiest way to ensure an accurate alignment is to turn the mitre gauge upside down, loosen the adjusting knob, slide it into the groove on the tool table, and press it against the table edge (Illus. 3-149). Now, tighten the knob and adjust the pointer if necessary (Illus. 3-150).

Mitre Variations

Chart 3-17 will give you the right degree to set your mitre gauge or radial arm saw to make mitres with different numbers of sides.

NO. OF SIDES	DEGREE OF CUT
3	60
4	45
5	36
6	30
7	25.7
8	22.5
9	20
10	18

Chart 3-17.

Motor Tool

The Sears Craftsman® motor tool shown in Illus. 3-151

will be a tremendous addition to any workshop. Dremel also has a number of motor tools. These tools are extremely useful for getting into tight corners when refinishing furniture, sanding minute detail work, cutting off bent nails, repairing screw heads, wood carving, and performing many other tasks. There are approximately 200 attachments available, from buffing wheels to saw blades. There is even an attachment that converts the motor tool into a router, and one that turns it into a mini drill press.

Moulding Head

(See Shaper Head)

Nails

(Also see Nuts and Bolts)

Brads

Brads are similar to finishing nails, but are thinner and have smaller heads. Brads are referred to by the inch size rather than by pennyweight. Brads are hard to find these days, because most woodworkers are using finishing nails. Common brad sizes are: ⅜, ½, ⅝, ¾, 1, 1¼, and 1½ inches.

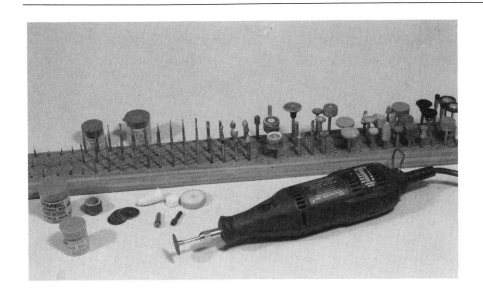

Illus. 3-151. The Sears Crafts-man® motor tool and attach-ments.

Common Nails

Chart 3-18 indicates the length and quantity per pound for different sizes of nails. *Note:* A 10-pennyweight nail is referred to as ten-penny nail and is written 10d. The quantity/pound figures in the chart are approximations.

There is no pennyweight reference after 60. In most areas, common nails 6 inches and longer are referred to as spikes.

Chart 3-19 describes the types of nail shown in Illus. 3-152.

PENNYWEIGHT (SIZE)	LENGTH	QUANTITY/POUND	
2	1 inch	850	
3	1¼ inches	540	
4	1½ inches	290	
5	1¾ inches	250	
6	2 inches	165	
7	2¼ inches	150	
8	2½ inches	100	
9	2¾ inches	90	
10	3 inches	65	
12	3¼ inches	60	**Chart 3-18.**
16	3½ inches	45	
20	4 inches	30	
30	4½ inches	20	
40	5 inches	17	
50	5½ inches	13	
60	6 inches	10	
	7 inches	7	
	8 inches	5	
	9 inches	4	
	10 inches	3	
	12 inches	3	
	14 inches	2	

Chart 3-19.

NUMBER IN ILLUS. AND LENGTH OF NAIL	DESCRIPTION OF NAIL
1. 14 inches	bright-finish spike
2. 12 inches	spiral (ardox) spike, hot-dipped (galvanized)
3. 7 inches	eavestrough spike
4. 7 inches	eavestrough spike
5. 4 inches	bright nail
6. 4 inches	bright ardox
7. 4 inches	bright, double-headed nail
8. 3½ inches	stainless ring nail
9. 3½ inches	bright nail
10. 3½ inches	phosphate-coated box nail
11. 3½ inches	electroplated ardox box nail
12. 3½ inches	hot-dipped ardox
13. 3 inches	aluminum nail
14. 2½ inches	bright nail
15. 2½ inches	bright ardox
16. 2½ inches	concrete nail
17. 2¼ inches	bright nail
18. 2¼ inches	hot-dipped ardox siding
19. 2¼ inches	hot-dipped siding
20. 2 inches	bright ardox
21. 1½ inches	bright ardox
22. 1¼ inches	blued, ringed (annual) floor nail
23. 1¼ inches	stainless ringed floor nail
24. 1¼ inches	hot-dipped roofing nail
25. 1¼ inches	electroplated roofing nail
26. 1¼ inches	bright nail
27. 1 inch	bright nail
28. ⅝ inch	bright nail
29. ½ inch	bright nail
30. ½ inch	bright cigar-box nail
31. 1½ inches	bright staple
32. 1½ inches	hot-dipped staple
33. 5¾ inches	forged spike (antique)

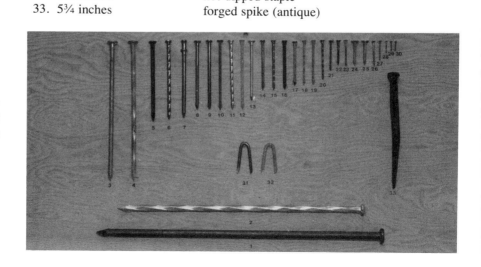

Illus. 3-152. Some of the commonly available nails. (Nails courtesy of Duchesne & Fils Ltée, Yamachiche, Québec, Canada)

Common Nail Characteristics

The common nail is probably one of the first metal fastening systems invented. It was and still is used for basic construction. It is rarely used for fine cabinetry, unless it is concealed in the inner framework. There are some forms of common nail used in finished work, but they usually have decorative heads as, for example, the upholstery nails used in Victorian furniture.

The common nail has undergone some radical changes over the centuries. Initially, common nails were made by hand, one nail at a time, by the village blacksmith. Then they were made square or flat, and had very little, if any, head on them. Eventually, machines were used to make nails. A truckload of nails could be produced in two days. The shape of the nail, though, remained the same.

Years later it was discovered that a round-shaped nail would hold much better and was easier to make because the nails would be cut from a large spool of wire. The thicker the wire, the longer the nail. From this discovery came the pennyweight system of describing a nail.

Through the years, engineers and architects have developed a multitude of different common nail types used for specific applications. There are nails designed to be used for underflooring, hardwood flooring, siding, roofing, casing, etc.

A relatively newcomer in the nailing business is the ardox, or spiral, nail. This nail is available as both a common and a finishing nail and has much more holding power than the round common nail. It is becoming much more prevalent in the construction industry.

There are five types of common nail head regularly used in construction. They are, as follow: 1. flat heads, used for basic construction; 2. wide flat heads such as found on roofing nails; 3. double-heads, for use in concrete forms or other construction that is to be dismantled;

4. oval heads, traditionally used for siding or shakes; and 5. a countersink head, for use on drywall.

Nails generally have one of four different types of points. They are, as follow: 1. the diamond point, the most common type; 2. soft or blunt points, which are used to secure hardwood flooring; 3. the needle point, which is used for fast assembly such as box or crate making; and 4. the chisel point, which is also used for fast assembly but in green wood. Chisel points will tend to hook when driven perpendicular to the grain.

Common nails have various finishes. Nails with a brilliant finish are the most common and are used on interior applications. Hot-dipped galvanized nails are used for exteriors or marine applications. Electroplated nails are used for interior but damp conditions and prevent oxidization. Phosphate nails will counteract the effects of the resin in green wood. Thermal-coated nails are used in hardwoods because they won't leave a black ring around the nail hole.

Finishing Nails, Hiding

This is an old method of hiding finishing nails that I learned way back in my school days in a woodworking class. With a very sharp ¼-inch wood chisel or a very sharp wood gouge, carefully lift, but don't remove, a small wedge on your workpiece (Illus. 3-153). Use a brad nailer to start your nail in the cavity. Carefully hammer it in, set it, and glue the lifted wedge back in place. Use masking tape to hold the glued wedge down, and remove all traces of glue seepage with a damp cloth.

If you are cutting into light-colored wood such as pine, use a painted (white) finishing nail to avoid any "see through." With hardwoods, raise the shaving along the figure line. Be extremely careful when doing this.

Illus. 3-153. An easy technique for hiding finishing nails.

A helpful tool that was designed just for this purpose is a Blind Nailer®. A Blind Nailer looks like a miniature surface planer. It's made by Veritas and is available from mail-order stores.

Finishing Nails Chart

Chart 3-20 indicates the length and quantity per pound for different sizes of nails.

Size of Nail

Before you drive that nail into your workpiece, think about the size of the nail that you are using. To achieve the strongest joint, the nail should penetrate two-thirds–three-quarters of the way into the second piece of wood (Illus. 3-155).

Nailing into Finished Wood

Sometimes finishing nails are required for the final assembly of your finished project. Hammering in finishing nails can be hazardous in that one slip of the hammer can result in a dimple that is very difficult to repair.

This technique will prevent a lot of frustration: place a shim or a piece of wood shingle on the part to be nailed and then simply drive the nail through the shim and into your workpiece (Illus. 3-156). When the nail is driven into the workpiece, just break off the shim and use a nail set to complete the job.

Chart 3-20.

PENNYWEIGHT (SIZE)	LENGTH	QUANTITY/POUND
2	1 inch	1050
3	1¼ inches	880
4	1½ inches	630
6	2 inches	290
8	2½ inches	195
10	3 inches	125
12	3¼ inches	88
16	3½ inches	77
20	4 inches	50

Note: The size of a finishing nail when written would be 2d for a 1-inch nail. Approximate numbers are given in the quantity/pound column in Chart 3-18.

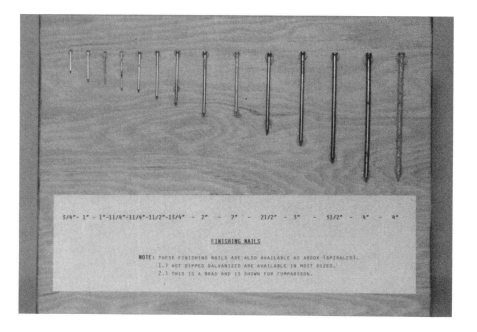

Illus. 3-154. Finishing nails.

Illus. 3-155. A strong joint will only be achieved if the nail penetrates two-thirds or three-quarters of the way into the second piece of wood.

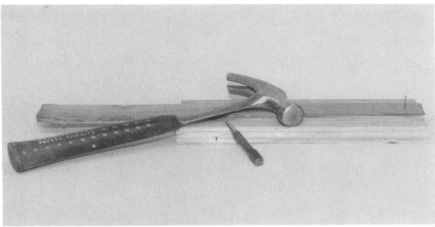

Illus. 3-156. When using finishing nails on your finished project, place a shim on the part to be nailed and then simply drive the nail through the shim and into the workpiece.

Setting Nails

Did you ever try setting a nail in a tight corner? The end result with a conventional nail set is usually a bent nail or a ding in the workpiece.

An offset nail-set tool does a good job of setting a nail in a tight corner (Illus. 3-157). It's inexpensive and available through the mail-order houses.

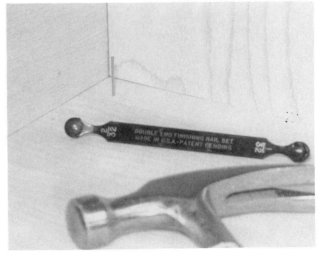

Illus. 3-157. This nail set does a good job of setting a nail in a tight corner.

Nail Sets

Illus. 3-158 shows different types of nail sets that you should have in your tool cabinet.

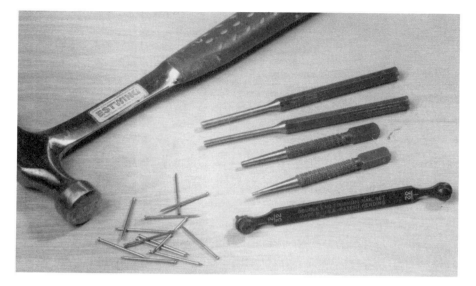

Illus. 3-158. Nail sets.

Nuts and Bolts, Sorting

Most woodworkers have a number of cans or other types of containers in their workshops which are overflowing with various-size nuts, bolts, screws, or nails. On some lazy Sunday afternoon between projects, go down to your workshop and start sorting them. Most hardware stores will probably have stackable mini-bins like the ones shown at Illus. 3-159 and 3-160 at a very reasonable price. They will save a great deal of time and frustration.

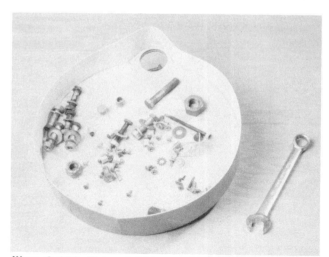

Illus. 3-159. This mini-bin can be used to store nuts and bolts.

Illus. 3-160. Storage facilities for nails and nuts.

The first thing to do after dumping the container's contents into the sorting tray is to throw away any screw, nut, or nail that is bent or damaged in any way. Next, start sorting the nuts, bolts, screws, or nails according to size and type.

When sorting nuts and bolts, screw the nut on the correct bolt and leave it there or just put the nut in an appropriate bin. Either way, it will save much time later.

Octagons

As defined by Webster's dictionary, an **octagon** is an eight-sided object with parallel sides that are equal. To make an octagonal chair or table leg, try using the following method: Take a piece of ¾ × ¾-inch scrap and cut it just slightly longer than the width of your table leg. Drill and then insert dowels in the ends as shown in Illus. 3-161. Divide the space between the dowels into thirds and drive two-inch finishing nails through the piece so that the points just protrude. You may want to use the drill press with a bit just slightly smaller than the nail. Hold the jig on your stock so that the dowels are firm against the sides and proceed to scribe down the length of the stock (Illus. 3-162). Now you can plane or cut along the lines to make your leg.

Oil

(See Lubricants)

Illus. 3-161. This jig can be used to scribe lines on stock or make octagonal chairs or table legs.

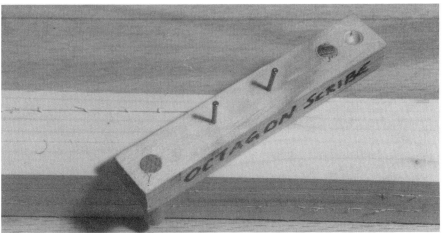

Illus. 3-162. Using the jigs to scribe down the length of the stock.

Oriented Strandboard (OSB)

(See Particleboard)

Paint

Storing Paint

Partially empty paint cans should be stored upside down (Illus. 3-163). This way, any skin that forms will be on the

Illus. 3-163. Store partially empty paint cans upside down. Make sure that the lids are on tight before inverting them.

bottom when you next open the can. The skin will usually support the weight of the paint on top of it, so mix it thoroughly but avoid breaking the skin. Also, make sure that the lids are on tight before inverting the paint cans.

There is another way to store partially empty cans of paint. Place a plastic shopping bag over the can. Put the top on over the plastic and hammer it on tight. Then, with a pair of scissors or a utility knife cut away the excess bag (Illus. 3-164 and 3-165). This will not only make a better seal, but it will prevent the paint from splashing on you when you hammer on the cover.

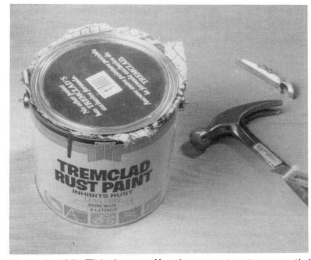

Illus. 3-164. Cutting away the excess bag.

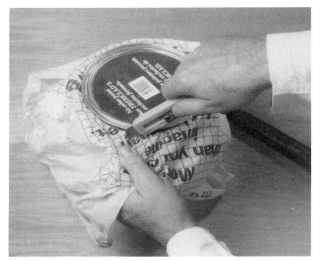

Illus. 3-165. This is an effective way to store partial cans of paints.

Using Old Paintbrushes

You can make use of old paintbrushes by removing their bristles and metal casings. You are now left with a handle that can be used to spread glue or, if you insert a piece of sheetmetal, as a scraper or spatula (Illus. 3-166). Some imagination is all that is required.

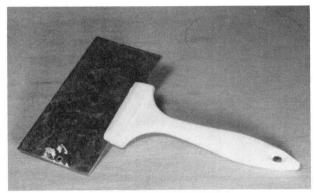

Illus. 3-166. By inserting a piece of sheetmetal into an old paintbrush handle, you have a tool that can be used to spread glue or as a scraper or spatula.

Filtering Paint

From your handy hardware store buy a yard or two of nylon window screening like the kind you find on those aluminum storm doors. Cut a piece just a little larger than your paint can, cut it in half, remove the lid, and tape the piece to the can (Illus. 3-167). An alternate method is cut a piece to fit over the deep end of your roller tray. Now, pour the paint into the tray. If the screen is on the paint can, leave it there but put the cover back on to prevent the paint from drying out. If the screen is on the roller tray, carefully remove and dispose of the screen. This will ensure that any skin or blobs of paint don't get on your brush or roller. It's not necessary to do this with a new can of paint, just with the ones that have been sitting around the basement for a year or two and are only partially full.

Making Your Own Paint

Years ago a paint called milk paint was made by the settlers and pioneers because it was cheap and lasted for a long time. Milk paint is back in vogue because of the new interest in antiques. Some of the craftspeople now use it. You can buy the powder premixed if you want, but it's expensive. Besides, there is some satisfaction in making your own.

Illus. 3-167. This piece of nylon window screening, taped to the can, can be used to filter paint.

To make your own milk paint, take an old but clean paint can and pour about a quart of water into it (Illus. 3-168). Set it on the stove and bring it close to a boil. Now, add about 10 or 12 ounces of non-fat powdered dry milk, stirring constantly until the mixture is the consistency of a thick soup. Slowly add a tube of *latex* tinting color until you have attained the desired shade. This tinting color is readily available at paint stores. If the paint is too dark, add more water. If it is too light, add more tint.

Milk paint should be applied with a soft brush or a soft, lint-free cloth. Be sure to keep the paint warm while applying it. Once it starts to dry, rub it in with a damp cloth. The more you wipe, the more transparent it becomes. Also, make sure that the surface you are painting is clean and there is no residue from old paint or varnish. Milk paint has to soak into the surface.

Painting Small Objects

It is almost impossible to paint a small drawer handle without getting paint all over your hands. To prevent this from happening, place a piece of double-face tape on your paint table and then stick the small parts (drawer handles, knobs, etc.) onto the tape (Illus. 3-169). This will prevent them from moving around as you carefully paint them.

Mixing Paint

Although there are many different types of paint mixers on the market, this method is equally effective. I use an old

Illus. 3-168. The ingredients needed to make milk paint.

Illus. 3-169. To prevent small parts from moving while you are painting them, stick them to the double-face tape on your paint table.

beater from a Mix-Master® (Illus. 3-170). This beater is installed in my portable *variable-speed* drill. Starting off very slowly, I gradually increase its speed until the paint is mixed thoroughly. Let the paint drip off the beater, put the beater in thinner or water (depending on the paint), and turn it on again for cleaning.

When mixing paint with your portable drill, get a lid from a plastic ice cream container that is large enough to cover the top of your paint can. Drill a hole large enough for the beater shaft to fit through, cover the paint can, and start mixing. This will prevent any chance of splattering.

Illus. 3-170 (right). This old beater makes an effective means of mixing paint.

Pouring Paint

Stick a piece of wide masking tape to the inside of the inner rim of a new can of paint (Illus. 3-171). (You may have to wipe it dry first.) The tape should be about 4 inches long and 2 inches wide. This will make a spout that will keep the inner rim and the outside of the can nearly paint-free (Illus. 3-172).

Spraying Paint

Here's a neat, simple way to make your own mini spray booth: Cut two flaps off an appropriate-size cardboard carton. The parts with the remaining flaps should be the top and bottom of the booth. Set your workpiece inside and paint it (Illus. 3-173). The upper flap of the carton may be trimmed or taped back if it gets in the way, but it is there to help prevent any overspray from leaving the box. It won't stop it all, so wear gloves and a shop coat.

Illus. 3-171. This piece of masking tape fixed to the inside of the rim of the paint can makes a good spout.

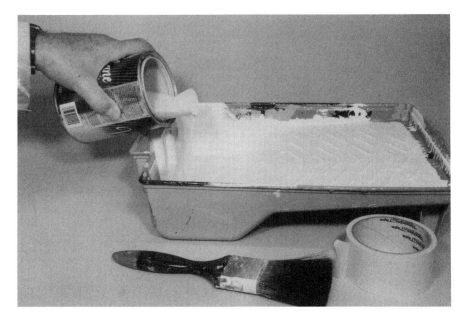

Illus. 3-172. This spout is very effective.

Illus. 3-173. This cardboard carton can be used as a spraying booth.

Panelling, Cutting

When installing thin (³⁄₁₆-inch) panelling, there are areas where you have to cut the panelling out to make room for switch boxes, receptacles, etc. In such case, try using an

Olfa®-type knife instead of drilling holes in the corners and then cutting them out with a portable jigsaw (Illus. 3-174). You will have to make a number of cuts to penetrate it with the knife, but if you make the first cut a light one, then the knife will have a tendency to follow that line. This makes for much neater cuts, and the panelling won't bounce around as it does with a saw.

Panel-Raising

(See Radial Arm Saw)

Particleboard, Characteristics and Uses

Particleboard is a panel that is comprised of a combination of wood flakes, chips, and shavings (Illus. 3-175). These pieces are compressed and combined with a resinous material and formed into sheets. The sheets vary in size,

Illus. 3-174. Use an Olfa®-type knife to cut thin panelling.

Illus. 3-175. Particleboard.

the most common being the standard 4×8-foot size. Other sizes that are available are 4×10 feet, 4×12 feet, 5×8 feet, 5×10 feet, and 5×12 feet.

Particleboard is available in various densities. The higher the density, the more impervious the particleboard is to water. The higher-density particleboard should be used for core material such as tabletops or countertops. As in plywood, both surfaces should be laminated to prevent warping.

Lower-density particleboard is used for such things as sheathing and sub-flooring. Like plywood, particleboard has dimensional stability and may be cut, routed, dadoed, and shaped with conventional power or hand tools. Carbide-tipped blades are, however, recommended.

Use pilot holes when using screws on particleboard. Particleboard will accept most glues. Nailing is acceptable, but I recommend the use of spiral nails.

A relatively new product on the market is called *OSB* (Illus. 3-176). OSB is oriented strandboard. Short wood strands are aligned along the length of the panel to give the finished product longitudinal strength for specific applications. It can also be made with layers of strands in a ply running at right angles to the next ply to give strength in both directions.

Waferboard, like OSB, is made from solid logs. No waste products are used. Waferboard is produced from randomly placed hardwood wafers and bonded with waterproof resins under heat and pressure. The result is a strong and stable panel.

Chipboard is an entirely different material than OSB and waterboard. Chipboard *is* made from waste products and is not as strong as the other materials. Chipboard will disintegrate if used for exterior applications.

Patterns

Drawing Patterns

Drawing a pattern for cutting on pine, spruce, or oak with a lead pencil makes it easy to see. Drawing a pattern on walnut or rosewood with the same pencil makes it a lot more difficult to see. To make the pencil line easier to see, outline it with a yellow wax pencil (Illus. 3-177). This will highlight the pencil line, making it much more visible, and will not damage the wood.

Illus. 3-176. Oriented strandboard.

Illus. 3-177. Outlining your pencil line with a yellow wax pencil will highlight it.

Transferring Patterns

Instead of transferring patterns from a project book onto paper or even directly onto your workpiece, buy a couple of sheets of white polystyrene from your local plastics dealer. They come in various thicknesses (gauges), so buy a thickness that can be easily cut with a pair of scissors or a utility knife.

Now, photocopy your pattern and stick it onto the polystyrene with double-face tape or rubber cement. Then cut it out with a utility knife (Illus. 3-178).

Lightly sand the rough spots off the edges with very fine sandpaper. Adhere the pattern to your workpiece with double-face tape and trace around it with a sharp pencil (Illus. 3-179).

When you are done, write a description of the pattern on the pattern itself with a soft-tip marker, drill a hole in the pattern, and hang it up for future use.

Illus. 3-178. Cut out the pattern with a utility knife.

Illus. 3-179. Trace around the pattern with a sharp pencil.

Pegboard, Description and Uses

Pegboard is an absolute must for every home workshop. After securing your pegboard to a frame of 1 × 2s to keep if away from the wall, nail or screw the panel in its desired place. Using the appropriate hooks, start hanging your tools (Illus. 3-180). *Do not* consider your first setup to be your last. You will find after a couple of days, or even weeks, that the positioning of the various tools is not convenient or to your liking. Only after you have become accustomed to the layout, and can easily locate that particular tool you need, can you consider the layout final.

Now, using a black (or any color) soft-tip marker, trace around all the tools and other paraphernalia. By doing this, it will become obviously apparent if something is missing on the board.

If your friends, neighbors, and family members are quick to borrow tools but slow to return them, hang a little note on the hook of the borrowed tool to remind you who has it (Illus. 3-181). If the paper starts to turn yellow, it's time to go looking for the tool.

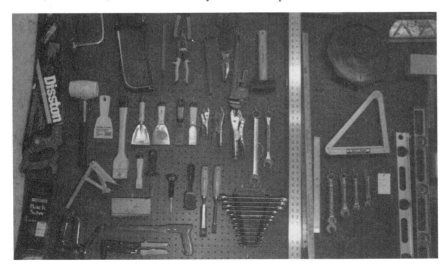

Illus. 3-180. Hang your tools on pegboard.

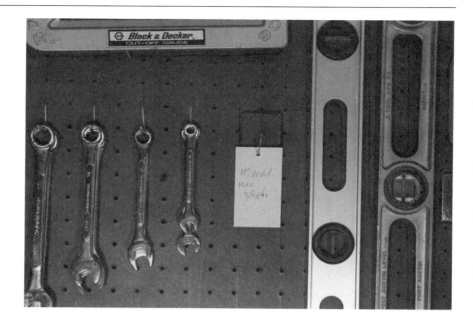

Illus. 3-181. When someone borrows a tool, hang a note on the hook of the borrowed tool to remind you who has it.

Plastics, Cutting

To cut Plexiglas®, polystyrene, and most other plastics up to ¼ inch thick, score the plastic lightly at first with a scratch awl or other sharp-pointed tool (Illus. 3-182). Then repeat the scoring a couple of times using progressively heavier pressure. Align the scribed mark on the edge of your workbench with the scribed face up (Illus. 3-183). Now, holding it securely, bend the material down until it snaps (Illus. 3-184). Practice this a couple of times on some scrap material before trying it on your workpiece.

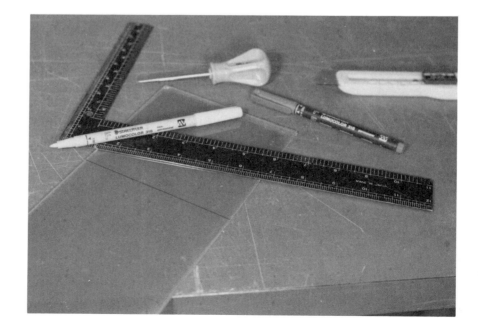

Illus. 3-182. Score the plastic with a sharp-pointed tool.

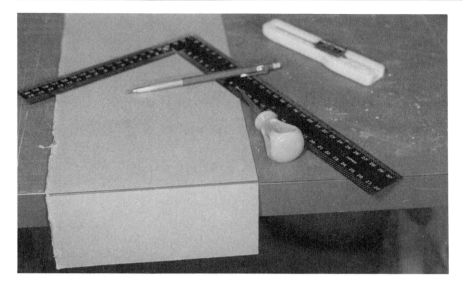

Illus. 3-183. Align the scribed mark on the edge of your workbench.

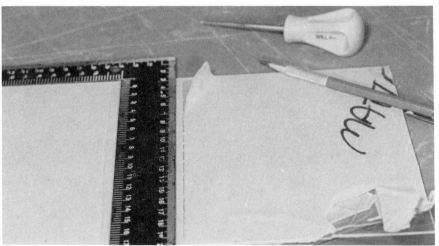

Illus. 3-184. Bend the material down until it snaps.

Plexiglas®, Working with

Plexiglas is fun to work with (Illus. 3-185). You can saw, drill, rout, bend, and sand it. Here are a few tips that you may want to follow when working with this material.

1. Never store Plexiglas in direct sunlight. The protective paper that's on it will dry up and become difficult to remove.
2. Leave the protective paper on until your project is finished. This will help prevent scratches to the surface.

3. Almost any drill bit may be used on Plexiglas, as long as it is sharp. Make sure, though, that you have a piece of scrap wood under it and that you drill *very* slowly, using light pressure.
4. You can cut Plexiglas with a band saw, but use a blade with the most teeth to the inch. When using a circular saw, also use a blade with the most teeth.
5. Plexiglas can be bent in boiling water, in an oven set at low heat, or with an electric bender. An electric bender is a tool with two heating elements. Place the Plexiglas between the two heating elements, wait a moment, and then bend the Plexiglas. Plexiglas gets very hot when the above methods are used, so be very careful when handling it. The protective paper should be removed before heating.
6. Sand the edges of Plexiglas with fine sandpaper or

Illus. 3-185. Cutting Plexiglas with a radial arm saw.

Illus. 3-186. Sanding the edge of Plexiglas with fine sandpaper.

emery cloth (Illus. 3-186). To get a clear edge on the plastic, sand the edge and then run a flame over it. Do this with a propane blowtorch (Illus. 3-187). Make light, frequent passes along the edges. Try this out on scrap before doing your workpiece. If the Plexiglas starts to ignite, blow it out immediately or douse it in water. *This operation should be performed outdoors or in a well-ventilated area!*

An easy way to remove the protective paper is to start at one corner. Then start rolling the paper off with a broom handle or a dowel, depending on the size of the piece. If the material has been cut, the edges of the paper may tend to stick, so proceed slowly.

Join Plexiglas with an acrylic solvent applied through a hypodermic needle (Illus. 3-188). Be careful; the needle is sharp. Don't let the solvent stay in the needle too long. Any remaining solvent should be put back in the bottle.

The solvent will eat at the plunger seal. Use the solvent sparingly and be sure not to let any drip where you don't want it. Tape the joint with masking tape to secure it. Inject at the joint only enough to see it fill the joint. Practice with scraps first.

Sometimes when you work with Plexiglas you will find that the protective paper has been removed or that the supplier has used a blue poly protector. How do you mark the Plexiglas for measuring? A pencil won't do, and an awl will leave a scratch right where you don't want it. Try this technique: Your stationery store or art-supplies dealer has water-soluble overhead projection markers in a rainbow of colors and a variety of point sizes (Illus. 3-189). Get a couple of dark-colored ones with fine points. Now, make your lines. A little Windex® and a soft cloth will wipe away any errant marks.

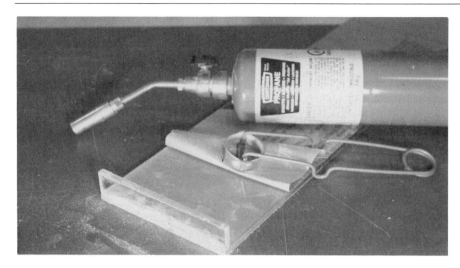

Illus. 3-187. Run a propane blowtorch over the edges of plastic, to get clear edges.

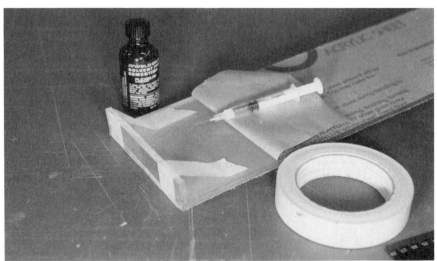

Illus. 3-188. Use a hypodermic needle to apply the acrylic solvent to the Plexiglas.

Illus. 3-189. Use a water-soluble overhead projection marker to mark Plexiglas.

Plywood

(Also see Hardboard and Particleboard)

Types, Grades, and Uses of Plywood

Chart 3-21 contains information on the types of plywood found in Canada, as well as how it is graded and how it is used. It has been supplied by the Council of Forest Industries of British Columbia and is reprinted with their permission. Chart 3-22 contains the same type of information for American plywood. This information has been supplied by the American Plywood Association.

Proven Performance

The Council of Forest Industries of British Columbia represents 10 member companies operating plywood mills throughout the province. Together, they account for the production of a significant proportion of all coniferous plywood manufactured in Canada.

Council members produce Douglas Fir plywood (DFP) and Canadian Softwood plywood (CSP) that meets the stringent quality requirements of the Canadian national standards CSA O121-M1978 Douglas Fir Plywood and CSA O151-M1978 Canadian Softwood Plywood. As well, COFI plywood producers must meet additional quality requirements set by COFI under a nationally accredited quality control program that includes regular mill inspections and laboratory testing.

The certified registration marks shown below appear on all regular grades of COFI plywood and are an assurance to the buyer of high quality and consistent performance.

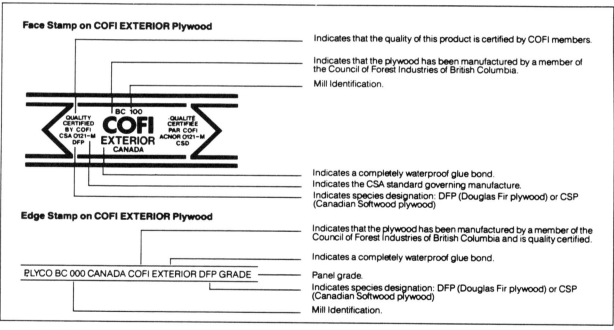

Face Stamp on COFI EXTERIOR Plywood

— Indicates that the quality of this product is certified by COFI members.

— Indicates that the plywood has been manufactured by a member of the Council of Forest Industries of British Columbia.

— Mill Identification.

— Indicates a completely waterproof glue bond.
— Indicates the CSA standard governing manufacture.
— Indicates species designation: DFP (Douglas Fir plywood) or CSP (Canadian Softwood plywood)

Edge Stamp on COFI EXTERIOR Plywood

— Indicates that the plywood has been manufactured by a member of the Council of Forest Industries of British Columbia and is quality certified.

— Indicates a completely waterproof glue bond.

PLYCO BC 000 CANADA COFI EXTERIOR DFP GRADE — Panel grade.
— Indicates species designation: DFP (Douglas Fir plywood) or CSP (Canadian Softwood plywood)
— Mill Identification.

Panel Thicknesses

Sheathing and Select Grades		Sanded Grades	
7.5 mm	20.5 mm	6 mm	19 mm
9.5 mm	22.5 mm	8 mm	21 mm
12.5 mm	25.5 mm	11 mm	24 mm
15.5 mm	28.5 mm	14 mm	27 mm
18.5 mm	31.5 mm	17 mm	30 mm

All thicknesses are metric. Some, but not all, thicknesses approximate imperial dimensions, namely: 6 mm (1/4''), 9.5 mm (3/8''), 12.5 mm (1/2''), 15.5 mm (5/8''), and 19 mm (3/4'').

A Choice of Panel Sizes

Square Edge	Tongue and Groove	COFI-ROOF
48 x 96 in. (1220 x 2440 mm)	1220 x 2440 mm	1220 x 2440 mm
48 x 108 in. (special order)	net face width 1207 mm	net face width 1205 mm
48 x 120 in. (special order)		
1200 x 2400 mm (special order)	1200 x 2400 mm	1200 x 2400 mm
1250 x 2500 mm (special order)	net face width 1187 mm	net face width 1185 mm

Chart 3-21 (here and page 135). Information concerning the types, grades, and uses of plywood in Canada. (Courtesy of Council of Forest Industries of British Columbia)

Guide to Canadian COFI EXTERIOR Plywood

COFI EXTERIOR Plywood Grades

Grade*	Specify By**	Veneer Grades			Characteristics	Typical Applications
		Face	Inner Plies	Back		
Good Two Sides (G2S)	CSA O121	A	C	A	Sanded. Best appearance both faces. May contain neat wood patches, inlays or synthetic patching material.	Furniture, cabinet doors, partitions, shelving, concrete forms, opaque paint finishes.
Good One Side (G1S)	CSA O121	A	C	C	Sanded. Best appearance one side only. May contain neat wood patches, inlays or synthetic patching material.	Where appearance or smooth sanded surface of one face is important. Cabinets, shelving, concrete forms.
Select – Tight Face (SEL TF)	CSA O121 or	B†	C	C	Unsanded. Permissible surface openings filled. May be cleaned and sized.	Underlayment and combined subfloor and underlayment. Hoarding. Construction use where sanded material is not required.
Select (SELECT)	CSA O151	B	C	C	Unsanded. Uniform surface with minor open splits. May be cleaned and sized.	
Sheathing (SHG)	CSA O121 or CSA O151	C	C	C	Unsanded. Face may contain limited size knots, knotholes and other minor defects.	Roof, wall, and floor sheathing. Hoarding. Construction use where sanded material or uniform surface not required.

COFI EXTERIOR Plywood Products

Product*	Specify By**	Veneer Grades			Characteristics	Typical Applications
		Face	Inner Plies	Back		
COFIFORM and COFIFORM PLUS	CSA O121 (with additional limits on thickness and species of face and inner plies)	A A B C	C C C C	A C C C	Special construction Douglas Fir panels with greater stiffness and strength providing improved properties particularly in wet service conditions. Available in regular sanded and unsanded grades and specialty grades with resin-fibre overlays or surface coatings of epoxy resin, modified polyurethanes or other proprietary compositions. Also available with factory-applied release agent.	Concrete forms and other uses where wet service conditions or superior strength requirements are encountered.
COFI-ROOF™	CSA O121 or CSA O151	B C	C C	C C	Unsanded. Face may contain limited size knots, knotholes and other minor defects. Milled with a patented edge profile for easy installation and edge support without H-clips.	Roof sheathing and decking for residential, commercial and industrial construction.
High Density Overlaid (HDO -O/-O)	CSA O121 or CSA O151	B†	C	B†	Smooth resin-fibre overlaid surface. Further finishing not required.	Bins, tanks, boats, furniture, signs, displays, forms for architectural concrete.
Medium Density Overlaid (Specify one or both sides) (MDOS1S, MDOS2S)	CSA O121 or CSA O151	C†	C	C†	Smooth resin-fibre overlaid surface. Best paint base.	Siding, soffits, panelling, built-in fitments, signs, any use requiring superior paint surface.

* All products including overlays bonded with waterproof resin glue.
** For complete grade descriptions see CSA O121 - M1978 and CSA O151 - M1978.
† Permissible openings filled.

Chart 3-21 continued.

Common Hardwood Plywood Grades

Designation	Description	Grade of Veneer		Characteristics
		Face	Back	
G/So	Good/Sound	#1 Face	Sound/Solid	Face veneer is book matched, allowing natural colour, limited natural characteristics and minimal defects. G/So back provides a solid surface. Generally used for high quality cabinetry where a natural finish is preferred.
G1S	Good One Side	#1 Face	Backing	
So2S	Sound Two Sides	Sound	Sound/Solid	Matching is not a requirement of the grade, allowing natural colour, increased natural characteristics and some defects. Generally used in less exposed areas where matched veneers are not important. The surface may be finished with stain or paint.
So1S	Sound One Side	Sound	Backing	
IND 2S	Industrial 2 Sides	Solid	Solid	Matching is not a requirement, and veneers allow most natural characteristics including minor repairs. Panels are generally used for utility purposes, usually with a paint finish.
IND 1S	Industrial 1 Side	Solid	Backing	

NOTE: G/So is available in Select Red and Select White which are book matched. Also Uniform red and Uniform white grades which have a pleasing match. So2S and So1S are available in red and white (birch and maple only).

TYPICAL APA SANDED PLYWOOD TRADEMARKS

TYPICAL BACKSTAMP

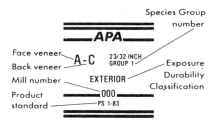

TYPICAL EDGEMARK

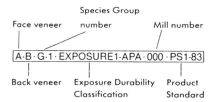

SPECIFICATIONS

GRADE DESIGNATIONS

Most sanded plywood grades are identified by the veneer grade used on the face and back of the panel, for example. A-C, B-D, etc. (See Table 1.)

Veneer grades define veneer quality according to natural unrepaired growth characteristics and allowable number and size of repairs permitted during manufacture. (See Table 2.) Veneer grades, in descending order of quality, are A, B, C-Plugged, C and D.[1] The minimum grade of veneer permitted in Exterior plywood is C. Use of D-grade veneer is limited to backs and inner plies of Exposure 1 or Interior panels.

Sanded plywood has B-grade or better veneer on one or both sides. Panels with B-grade or better veneer on both sides usually carry the APA trademark on the panel edge. Otherwise, the trademark is stamped on the back of the panel. Typical APA sanded plywood trademarks (edgemarks and backstamps) are illustrated and explained at left.

EXPOSURE DURABILITY CLASSIFICATIONS

Sanded plywood is produced in three basic exposure durability classifications: Exterior, Exposure 1 and Interior.

Exterior panels are made with a fully waterproof bond and are designed for applications subject to permanent exposure to the weather or moisture.

Exposure 1 panels have a fully waterproof bond and are designed for applications where long delays may be expected prior to providing protection, or where high moisture conditions may be encountered in service. Exposure 1 panels are made with the same exterior adhesives used in Exterior panels. However, because other compositional factors may affect glueline performance, only Exterior panels should be used for permanent exposure to the weather.

Interior panels lacking additional glueline information in their trademarks are manufactured with interior glue and are intended for interior applications only.

SPECIES GROUPS

Plywood can be manufactured from over 70 species of wood under *U.S. Product Standard PS 1-83 for Construction and Industrial Plywood*. These species are divided according to strength and stiffness

Chart 3-22 (here and pages 137–146). Information on American plywood.

into five groups – Groups 1 through 5. Group 1 species are the strongest and stiffest, Group 2 the next strongest, and so on. (See Table 3.)

The Group number in the APA trademark of sanded plywood refers to the species used for face and back veneers. When face and back veneers are from different species, the higher Group number is used.[2]

PANEL SIZE AND THICKNESS

Standard sanded plywood dimensions are 48 inches by 96 inches, although some manufacturers are equipped to produce longer and wider panels. Common thicknesses are 1/4, 9/32, 11/32, 3/8, 15/32, 1/2, 19/32, 5/8, 23/32, and 3/4 inch.

HOW TO ORDER

To order sanded plywood, designate the thickness, APA trademark, grade, Group number, exposure durability classification, dimensions, and number of pieces. For example:

3/4″ APA A-C, Group 1, Exterior, 48″x96″, 100 pcs.

TABLE 1
GUIDE TO APA SANDED PLYWOOD GRADES[1][2]

A·A·G·1·EXPOSURE1·APA·000·PS1·83

APA A-A

Use where appearance of both sides is important for interior applications such as built-ins, cabinets, furniture, partitions; and exterior applications such as fences, signs, boats, shipping containers, tanks, ducts, etc. Smooth surfaces suitable for painting. EXPOSURE DURABILITY CLASSIFICATIONS: Interior, Exposure 1, Exterior. COMMON THICKNESSES: 1/4, 11/32, 3/8, 15/32, 1/2, 19/32, 5/8, 23/32, 3/4.

A·B·G·1·EXPOSURE1·APA·000·PS1·83

APA A-B

For use where appearance of one side is less important but where two solid surfaces are necessary. EXPOSURE DURABILITY CLASSIFICATIONS: Interior, Exposure 1, Exterior. COMMON THICKNESSES: 1/4, 11/32, 3/8, 15/32, 1/2, 19/32, 5/8, 23/32, 3/4.

APA
A-C   GROUP 1
EXTERIOR
000
PS 1-83

APA A-C

For use where appearance of only one side is important in exterior applications such as soffits, fences, structural uses, boxcar and truck linings, farm buildings, tanks, trays, commercial refrigerators, etc.[3] EXPOSURE DURABILITY CLASSIFICATION: Exterior. COMMON THICKNESSES: 1/4, 9/32, 11/32, 3/8, 15/32, 1/2, 19/32, 5/8, 23/32, 3/4.

APA
A-D   GROUP 1
EXPOSURE 1
000
PS 1-83

APA A-D

For use where appearance of only one side is important in interior applications, such as paneling, built-ins, shelving, partitions, flow racks, etc.[3] EXPOSURE DURABILITY CLASSIFICATIONS: Interior, Exposure 1. COMMON THICKNESSES: 1/4, 9/32, 11/32, 3/8, 15/32, 1/2, 19/32, 5/8, 23/32, 3/4.

B·B·G·2·EXPOSURE1·APA·000·PS1·83

APA B-B

Utility panels with two solid sides. EXPOSURE DURABILITY CLASSIFICATIONS: Interior, Exposure 1, Exterior. COMMON THICKNESSES: 1/4, 11/32, 3/8, 15/32, 1/2, 19/32, 5/8, 23/32, 3/4.

APA
B-C   GROUP 1
EXTERIOR
000
PS 1-83

APA B-C

Utility panel for farm service and work buildings, boxcar and truck linings, containers, tanks, agricultural equipment, as a base for exterior coatings and other exterior uses or applications subject to high or continuous moisture.[3] EXPOSURE DURABILITY CLASSIFICATION: Exterior. COMMON THICKNESSES: 1/4, 9/32, 11/32, 3/8, 15/32, 1/2, 19/32, 5/8, 23/32, 3/4.

(2) Panels 3/8-inch thick or less are identified by face species because they are chosen primarily for appearance and used in applications where structural properties are not critical. Panels thicker than 3/8 inch are identified by face species if C or D backs are at least 1/8-inch thick and are not more than one species group number higher than face species.

Chart 3-22 continued.

APA B-D

Utility panel for backing, sides of built-ins, industry shelving, slip sheets, separator boards, bins and other interior or protected applications.(3) EXPOSURE DURABILITY CLASSIFICATIONS: Interior, Exposure 1. COMMON THICKNESSES: 1/4, 9/32, 11/32, 3/8, 15/32, 1/2, 19/32, 5/8, 23/32, 3/4.

MARINE · A-A · EXT-APA · 000 · PS1-83

APA MARINE

Specially designed plywood panel made only with Douglas-fir or western larch, and highly restrictive limitations on core gaps and face repairs. Ideal for boat hulls and other marine applications where bending is involved. Also available with HDO or MDO faces. EXPOSURE DURABILITY CLASSIFICATION: Exterior. COMMON THICKNESSES: 1/4, 3/8, 1/2, 5/8, 3/4.

APA B-B PLYFORM CLASS I

APA proprietary concrete form panels designed for high reuse. Sanded both sides and mill-oiled unless otherwise specified. Class I, the strongest, stiffest and more commonly available, is limited to Group 1 faces, Group 1 or 2 crossbands, and Group 1, 2, 3, or 4 inner plies. (Plyform Class II, limited to Group 1, 2 or 3 faces under certain conditions and Group 1, 2, 3 or 4 inner plies, may also be available.) Also available in HDO for very smooth concrete finish, in Structural I, and with special overlays. EXPOSURE DURABILITY CLASSIFICATION: Exterior. COMMON THICKNESSES: 19/32, 5/8, 23/32, 3/4.

GRADE	THICKNESSES	Minimum Number of PLIES	Minimum Number of LAYERS(4)
APA A-A APA A-B APA A-C	1/4, 9/32, 11/32, 3/8	3	3
APA A-D APA B-B	15/32, 1/2	4	3
APA B-C APA B-D	19/32, 5/8, 23/32, 3/4	5	5
APA MARINE	1/4, 3/8	3	3
	1/2, 5/8, 3/4	5	5

(1) Exterior sanded panels can also be manufactured in Structural I (all plies limited to Group 1 species) and Structural II (all plies limited to Group 1, 2 or 3 species). Check availability before specifying.

(2) For information on touch-sanded plywood (such as Underlayment), contact APA.

(3) For nonstructural floor underlayment in areas to be covered with thin resilient (non-textile) floor covering, or other applications requiring improved inner-ply construction, specify panels marked ''plugged inner plies'' (also may be designated ''plugged crossbands under face'' or ''plugged crossbands (or core)'' or ''meets underlayment requirements'').

(4) A layer is a single veneer ply, or two or more plies laminated with grain direction parallel in each ply.

Chart 3-22 continued.

T A B L E 2
VENEER GRADES

N	Smooth surface "natural finish" veneer. Select, all heartwood or all sapwood. Free of open defects. Allows not more than 6 repairs, wood only, per 4 x 8 panel, made parallel to grain and well matched for grain and color.
A	Smooth, paintable. Not more than 18 neatly made repairs, boat, sled, or router type, and parallel to grain, permitted. May be used for natural finish in less demanding applications. Synthetic repairs permitted.
B	Solid surface. Shims, circular repair plugs and tight knots to 1 inch across grain permitted. Some minor splits permitted. Synthetic repairs permitted.
C Plugged	Improved C veneer with splits limited to 1/8-inch width and knotholes and borer holes limited to 1/4 x 1/2 inch. Admits some broken grain. Synthetic repairs permitted.
C	Tight knots to 1-1/2 inch. Knotholes to 1 inch across grain and some to 1-1/2 inch if total width of knots and knotholes is within specified limits. Synthetic or wood repairs. Discoloration and sanding defects that do not impair strength permitted. Limited splits allowed. Stitching permitted.
D	Knots and knotholes to 2-1/2-inch width across grain and 1/2 inch larger within specified limits. Limited splits are permitted. Stitching permitted. Limited to Exposure 1, or Interior panels.

T A B L E 3
CLASSIFICATION OF SPECIES

Group 1	Group 2		Group 3	Group 4	Group 5
Apitong	Cedar, Port	Maple, Black	Alder, Red	Aspen	Basswood
Beech,	Orford	Mengkulang	Birch, Paper	Bigtooth	Poplar,
American	Cypress	Meranti,	Cedar, Alaska	Quaking	Balsam
Birch	Douglas	Red (2)	Fir,	Cativo	
Sweet	Fir 2 (1)	Mersawa	Subalpine	Cedar	
Yellow	Fir	Pine	Hemlock,	Incense	
Douglas	Balsam	Pond	Eastern	Western	
Fir 1 (1)	California	Red	Maple,	Red	
Kapur	Red	Virginia	Bigleaf	Cottonwood	
Keruing	Grand	Western	Pine	Eastern	
Larch,	Noble	White	Jack	Black	
Western	Pacific	Spruce	Lodgepole	(Western	
Maple, Sugar	Silver	Black	Ponderosa	Poplar)	
Pine	White	Red	Spruce	Pine	
Caribbean	Hemlock,	Sitka	Redwood	Eastern	
Ocote	Western	Sweetgum	Spruce	White	
Pine, Southern	Lauan	Tamarack	Engelmann	Sugar	
Loblolly	Almon	Yellow-	White		
Longleaf	Bagtikan	Poplar			
Shortleaf	Mayapis				
Slash	Red				
Tanoak	Tangile				
	White				

(1) Douglas Fir from trees grown in the states of Washington, Oregon, California, Idaho, Montana, Wyoming, and the Canadian Provinces of Alberta and British Columbia shall be classed as Douglas Fir No. 1. Douglas Fir from trees grown in the states of Nevada, Utah, Colorado, Arizona and New Mexico shall be classed as Douglas Fir No. 2.
(2) Red Meranti shall be limited to species having a specific gravity of 0.41 or more based on green volume and oven dry weight.

Chart 3-22 continued.

PRODUCT FEATURES

APA trademarked sanded plywood offers numerous advantages as a structural and aesthetic construction material, including:

APPEARANCE

The high grade of sanded plywood face or face and back veneers provides a beautiful finish-quality surface for all kinds of applications, from cabinets and built-ins to soffits and paneling. And since it is sanded at the mill, little or no additional sanding is required for most applications.

STRENGTH AND STIFFNESS

By cross laminating layers of wood veneer, sanded plywood provides an excellent strength-to-weight ratio and exhibits superior stiffness along both the length and width of the panel. While sanded plywood, particularly thinner panels, is frequently used for appearance applications where structural properties are of little importance, it should be noted that sanded plywood is a structural material for which design stresses and section properties have been calculated and published. These data permit the product to be used for a wide variety of engineered construction and industrial applications where design values are required.

DIMENSIONAL STABILITY

Plywood's cross-laminated construction also provides superior dimensional stability, or resistance to warping or buckling in the plane of the panel when exposed to moisture. Wood tends to shrink much more across the grain than along the grain with changes in moisture content. In plywood, the tendency of

individual veneers to swell or shrink is greatly restricted by the relative longitudinal stability of the adjacent plies.

Plywood also is dimensionally stable in the plane of the panel when subjected to changing temperatures.

IMPACT RESISTANCE

Plywood improves on wood's well-known ability to absorb shock. Even when supported on only two edges, its cross-laminated construction and large panel size distribute impact loads. Impact load distribution is even greater when the panel is supported along all four edges.

CHEMICAL RESISTANCE

Exterior plywood exhibits excellent resistance to a wide range of chemicals, making it ideally suited for a number of demanding industrial applications. Plywood's strength is not significantly affected by organic chemicals, neutral and acid salts, or by most acids and alkalies in the pH range of 3 to 10. The chemical resistance of the phenolic resin glues used in Exterior plywood is at least as good, and generally better, than the wood itself.

Exposure 1 plywood has about the same chemical resistance as Exterior, but is not recommended for long-term exposure to moisture except in cases where some localized separation of veneers is acceptable.

FASTENER-HOLDING ABILITY

Due again to its cross-laminated construction, sanded plywood possesses excellent nail-holding ability. Nails can be placed near panel edges without splitting the panel.

Sanded plywood also can be attached

to steel or aluminum with mechanical fasteners. These commonly include self-drilling, self-tapping screws and hardened helically threaded nails which can be power or hand driven.

WORKABILITY

The ease with which sanded plywood can be cut, drilled, routed, jointed, glued, fastened and finished with ordinary tools and basic skills is another of its many advantages.

Support panels firmly with the best side up when hand sawing or when using a radial-arm or table saw. Cut with the best side down when using a portable power saw.

Plywood also can be die cut and stitched. Thicknesses up to and including 3/8 inch can be die cut with little difficulty. Some experience and specialized techniques are necessary to cut thicker panels. Grades with a minimum of defects provide the smoothest cut and Exterior panels are preferred to Exposure 1 or Interior panels. Fabric or plastic materials can be stitched to panels up to 3/8 inch thick with industrial sewing machines. Ultimate test values in excess of 100 pounds per lineal inch have been achieved with fabrics stitched to 1/4-inch-thick plywood.

AVAILABILITY

Sanded plywood is made by numerous American Plywood Association member manufacturers and is available in virtually every region of the country. Some grades, thicknesses and species are more commonly manufactured than others. Check with your supplier for local availability of the many sanded grades, thicknesses and species.

Chart 3-22 continued.

FINISHING RECOMMENDATIONS

INTERIOR APPLICATIONS

A wide variety of finishes are available on sanded plywood used for interior applications. The most common are described below. Always use finishes formulated for wood and follow the finish manufacturer's recommendations for best results. For interior (and exterior) applications, little or no sanding of the mill-sanded plywood surface is advised before application of the finish, to avoid uneven highlighting of hard and soft grain areas on the surface of the panels.

Natural Finishes. Various clear finishes and oils can be used on sanded plywood to provide the ever-popular real wood appearance. For the most natural effect, use two coats of a clear penetrating sealer. This type of finish resists soiling and allows easy cleaning. Some sealers can be tinted or used with light stains to add color and to produce a variety of attractive effects. Other clear finishes can also be used. Many finish manufacturers recommend that a sealer be used before applying a film-forming clear finish such as varnish.

Color Toning. Repairs and grain irregularities in sanded plywood can be pleasantly subdued by color toning. Tones of light gray, brown or tan go well with wood colors and provide the best masking. Two color toning techniques are recommended. The easiest method uses a heavy- bodied non-penetrating sealer containing non-hiding pigments, and companion stains for color. Tint a small amount of the sealer with stains until the desired tone is obtained on a panel sample. Then mix the same proportions

of stain and sealer in sufficient quantity for the entire job and apply by brush or spray. After drying and light sanding, apply a coat of clear finish to give the desired luster.

Where more control of the panel color differences is wanted, begin by whitening the surface with pigmented resin sealer or diluted interior white undercoat. Wipe off before becoming tacky to display the grain desired. Then apply a clear resin sealer, allow to dry, and sand lightly. Next, apply a light stain, pigmented sealer or tinted undercoat and wipe to the desired color depth.

After drying and light sanding, apply a coat of satin varnish or brushing lacquer to provide luster and durability.

Semitransparent Stains. Semitransparent stains are highly recommended where both color and show-through of the grain and natural wood characteristics are desired. When light colors are used, only oil-based semitransparent stains are recommended. These help prevent discoloration of the finish caused by natural water-soluble compounds (called extractives) in the wood.

Solid-color Stains and Paints (Including Enamels). These colored finishes, especially paint, are opaque and mask repairs and wood grain patterns. Paints typically provide a smoother surface than solid-color stains.

Paints are available in either oil-base or water-base (latex). Both normally require two coats, a primer or undercoat and a topcoat. The oil-based and darker colored latex solid-color stains often require only one coat. However, lighter colored latex stains usually require a stain-resistant

undercoat to prevent discoloration of the finish by extractives.

Paints are available in a full range of gloss levels, including flat, semigloss and gloss. The flat finishes are generally more difficult to clean when soiled.

EXTERIOR APPLICATIONS

Sanded plywood is not recommended as an exterior siding on most buildings. However, it is frequently used for soffits and miscellaneous other exterior uses. For these applications, only acrylic latex house paints are recommended.

House paints require at least two coats, a primer and topcoat. Primers are formulated specifically for controlled penetration, optimum bonding to the substrate, and minimal extractive staining. Some acrylic latex systems use oil or oil-alkyd primer followed by the acrylic latex topcoat. Other systems use one or two coats of a stain-blocking acrylic latex primer and generally offer superior performance. In any case, select companion products designed to be used together and preferably from the same manufacturer. Two topcoats will provide significant improvement in the life and performance of the finish.

Edge Treatment. All edges of plywood panels used for exterior applications should receive edge protection to minimize the effects of moisture absorption. Use the same exterior house paint primer for the edges that will be used on the face.

Chart 3-22 continued.

CARE AND HANDLING

Like all building materials, sanded plywood should be properly stored, handled and installed to assure superior in-service performance.

Protect the edges and ends of panels. While minor damage to panel edges and ends won't affect the structural capability of the panel, it can add to in-place repair costs. Place panels to be moved by forklift on pallets or bunks to avoid damage by fork tines.

Panels to be transported on open truckbeds should be covered with standard tarpaulins. For open railcar shipment, use "lumber wrap" to avoid extended weather exposure.

Store panels whenever possible under roof, especially if they won't be used soon after received. Keep panels away from open doorways and weight down the top panel in a stack to avoid any possible warpage from humidity. If moisture absorption is expected, cut steel banding on panel bundles to prevent edge damage. Use at least three full-width supports along the eight-foot length of the panel – one centered and the others 12 to 16 inches from each end.

If panels must be stored outside, special care should be taken to support and cover them. Stack panels on a level platform supported by 4x4 stringers or other blocking. Never leave panels or the platform in direct contact with the ground.

Cover the stack loosely with plastic sheets or tarps. Anchor the covering at the top of the stack, but keep it open and away from the sides and bottom to assure good ventilation. Tight coverings prevent air circulation and, when exposed to sunlight, create a "greenhouse" effect which may encourage mold formation.

Chart 3-22 continued.

KEY DEFINITIONS

TYPICAL APA REGISTERED TRADEMARKS

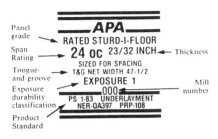

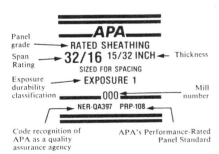

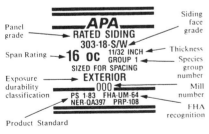

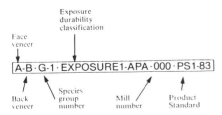

Chart 3-22 continued.

APA PERFORMANCE STANDARDS

APA performance standards are the result of new manufacturing technology that makes possible the manufacture of structural panel products from wood by-products and species not provided for in *U.S. Product Standard PS 1-83*. APA performance standards deal exclusively with how a product must perform in a designated application rather than from what or how the product must be manufactured.

Panels produced under APA performance standards — called APA Performance Rated Panels — must meet several performance baseline requirements according to the panel's designated end use. These performance requirements include uniform and concentrated static and impact load capacity, fastener-holding ability, racking resistance, dimensional stability, and bond durability.

In addition to conventional veneer plywood, APA performance standards encompass such other panel products as composites, waferboard and oriented strand board. (See APA Performance Rated Panels," page 8.)

For complete performance testing and qualification information, write APA for *PRP-108, Performance Standards and Policies for Structural-Use Panels*, Form E445.

GRADE

The term "grade" may refer to *panel* grade or to *veneer* grade. Panel grades are generally identified in terms of the veneer grade used on the face and back of the panel (e.g., A-B, B-C, etc.), or by a name suggesting the panel's intended end use (e.g., APA Rated Sheathing, Underlayment, etc.).

Veneer grades define veneer appearance in terms of natural unrepaired growth characteristics and allowable number and size of repairs that may be made during manufacture. The highest quality veneer is "A," [1] the lowest "D." The minimum grade of veneer permitted in Exterior plywood is "C." "D" veneer is used only in panels intended for interior use or for applications protected from permanent exposure to the weather.

EXPOSURE DURABILITY

APA trademarked panels may be produced in four exposure durability classifications — Exterior, Exposure 1, Exposure 2, and Interior.

Exterior panels have a fully water-proof bond and are designed for applications subject to permanent exposure to the weather or to moisture.

(1) Some manufacturers also produce a premium "N" grade (natural finish) veneer, available only on special order.

KEY DEFINITIONS

VENEER GRADES

A Smooth, paintable. Not more than 18 neatly made repairs, boat, sled, or router type, and parallel to grain, permitted. May be used for natural finish in less demanding applications. Synthetic repairs permitted.

B Solid surface. Shims, circular repair plugs and tight knots to 1 inch across grain permitted. Some minor splits permitted. Synthetic repairs permitted.

C Plugged Improved C veneer with splits limited to 1/8 inch width and knotholes and borer holes limited to 1/4 x 1/2 inch. Admits some broken grain. Synthetic repairs permitted.

C Tight knots to 1½ inch. Knotholes to 1 inch across grain and some to 1½ inch if total width of knots and knotholes is within specified limits. Synthetic or wood repairs. Discoloration and sanding defects that do not impair strength permitted. Limited splits allowed. Stitching permitted.

D Knots and knotholes to 2½ inch width across grain and 1/2 inch larger within specified limits. Limited splits allowed. Stitching permitted. Limited to Interior, Exposure 1 and Exposure 2 panels.

Exposure 1 panels have a fully waterproof bond and are designed for applications where long construction delays may be expected prior to providing protection, or where high moisture conditions may be encountered in service. Exposure 1 panels are made with the same exterior adhesives used in Exterior panels. However, because other compositional factors may affect bond performance, only Exterior panels should be used for permanent exposure to the weather.(2)

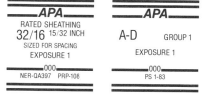

(2) Exposure 1 panels may be used when exposure to the outdoors is on the underside only, such as at roof overhangs.

Chart 3-22 continued.

NOTE: All-veneer APA Rated Sheathing Exposure 1, commonly called "CDX" in the trade, is frequently mistaken as an Exterior panel and erroneously used in applications for which it does not possess the required resistance to weather. "CDX" should only be used for applications as outlined under Exposure 1 above. For sheathing grade panels that will be exposed permanently to the weather, specify APA Rated Sheathing Exterior (C-C Exterior under PS 1.)

See Treated Plywood (page 18) for recommended plywood grades and exposure durability classifications in applications requiring fire-retardant-treated or preservative-treated plywood.

APA SPECIALTY PANELS

APA trademarked specialty grades include panels designed for specific applications (e.g., B-B Plyform for concrete forming, Marine), or with special surface treatments for applications with specific performance requirements (e.g., Medium and High Density Overlay, Plyron).

Complete concrete forming design data are contained in APA's *Concrete Forming*, Form V345. For additional information on High and Medium Density Overlay plywood, write for *HDO/MDO Plywood*, Form B360.

GUIDE TO APA SPECIALTY PANELS
Trademarks Shown Are Typical Facsimiles

```
HDO · A-A · G-1 · EXT-APA · 000 · PS1-83
```

APA HIGH DENSITY OVERLAY (HDO)

Plywood panel manufactured with a hard, semi-opaque resin-fiber overlay on both sides. Extremely abrasion resistant and ideally suited to scores of punishing construction and industrial applications, such as concrete forms, industrial tanks, work surfaces, signs, agricultural bins, exhaust ducts, etc. Also available with skid-resistant screen-grid surface and in Structural I. EXPOSURE DURABILITY CLASSIFICATION: Exterior. COMMON THICKNESSES: 3/8, 1/2, 5/8, 3/4.

```
MARINE · A-A · EXT-APA · 000 · PS1-83
```

APA MARINE

Specially designed plywood panel made only with Douglas-fir or western larch, solid jointed cores, and highly restrictive limitations on core gaps and face repairs. Ideal for boat hulls and other marine applications. Also available with HDO or MDO faces. EXPOSURE DURABILITY CLASSIFICATION: Exterior. COMMON THICKNESSES: 1/4, 3/8, 1/2, 5/8, 3/4.

```
___APA___
PLYFORM
B-B  CLASS I
EXTERIOR
___000___
PS 1-83
```

APA B-B PLYFORM CLASS I

APA proprietary concrete form panels designed for high reuse. Sanded both sides and mill-oiled unless otherwise specified. Special restrictions on species. Also available in HDO for very smooth concrete finish, in Structural I, and with special overlays. EXPOSURE DURABILITY CLASSIFICATION: Exterior. COMMON THICKNESSES: 19/32, 5/8, 23/32, 3/4.

```
___APA___
M. D. OVERLAY
GROUP 1
EXTERIOR
___000___
PS 1-83
```

APA MEDIUM DENSITY OVERLAY (MDO)

Plywood panel manufactured with smooth, opaque, resin-treated fiber overlay providing ideal base for paint on one or both sides. Excellent material choice for shelving, factory work surfaces, paneling, built-ins, signs and numerous other construction and industrial applications. Also available as Rated Siding 303 with texture-embossed or smooth surface on one side only and in Structural I. EXPOSURE DURABILITY CLASSIFICATION: Exterior. COMMON THICKNESSES: 11/32, 3/8, 15/32, 1/2, 19/32, 5/8, 23/32, 3/4.

```
___APA___
DECORATIVE
GROUP 2
INTERIOR
___000___
PS 1-83
```

APA DECORATIVE

Rough sawn, brushed, grooved, or other faces. For paneling, interior accent walls, built-ins, counter facing, exhibit displays, etc. Made by some manufacturers in Exterior for exterior siding, gable ends, fences and other exterior applications. Use recommendations for Exterior panels vary; check with the manufacturer. EXPOSURE DURABILITY CLASSIFICATIONS: Interior, Exposure 1, Exterior. COMMON THICKNESSES: 5/16, 3/8, 1/2, 5/8.

```
PLYRON · EXPOSURE1-APA · 000
```

APA PLYRON

APA proprietary plywood panel with hardboard face on both sides. Faces tempered, untempered, smooth or screened. For countertops, shelving, cabinet doors, concentrated load flooring, etc. EXPOSURE DURABILITY CLASSIFICATIONS: Interior, Exposure 1, Exterior. COMMON THICKNESSES: 1/2, 5/8, 3/4.

Chart 3-22 continued.

APA SANDED & TOUCH-SANDED PLYWOOD

APA
B-C GROUP 1
EXTERIOR
_000_
PS 1-83

APA
B-D GROUP 2
INTERIOR
_000_
PS 1-83

APA
UNDERLAYMENT
GROUP 1
EXPOSURE 1
_000_
PS 1-83

APA B-C

Utility panel for farm service and work buildings, boxcar and truck linings, containers, tanks, agricultural equipment, as a base for exterior coatings and other exterior uses.[1] EXPOSURE DURABILITY CLASSIFICATION: Exterior. COMMON THICKNESSES: 1/4, 11/32, 3/8, 15/32, 1/2, 19/32, 5/8, 23/32, 3/4.

APA B-D

Utility panel for backing, sides of built-ins, industry shelving, slip sheets, separator boards, bins and other interior or protected applications.[1] EXPOSURE DURABILITY CLASSIFICATIONS: Interior, Exposure 1. COMMON THICKNESSES: 1/4, 11/32, 3/8, 15/32, 1/2, 19/32, 5/8, 23/32, 3/4.

APA UNDERLAYMENT

For application over structural subfloor. Provides smooth surface for application of carpet and possesses high concentrated and impact load resistance. Touch sanded. For areas to be covered with resilient non-textile flooring, specify panels with "sanded face".[2] EXPOSURE DURABILITY CLASSIFICATIONS: Interior, Exposure 1. COMMON THICKNESSES[4]: 1/4, 11/32, 3/8, 1/2, 19/32, 5/8, 23/32, 3/4.

APA
C-C PLUGGED
GROUP 2
EXTERIOR
_000_
PS 1-83

APA
C-D PLUGGED
GROUP 2
EXPOSURE 1
_000_
PS 1-83

APA C-C PLUGGED[3]

For use as an underlayment over structural subfloor, refrigerated or controlled atmosphere storage rooms, pallet fruit bins, tanks, boxcar and truck floors and linings, and other exterior applications. Provides smooth surface for application of carpet and possesses high concentrated and impact load resistance. Touch-sanded. For areas to be covered with resilient non-textile flooring, specify panels with "sanded face." EXPOSURE DURABILITY CLASSIFICATION: Exterior. COMMON THICKNESSES[4]: 11/32, 3/8, 1/2, 19/32, 5/8, 23/32, 3/4.

APA C-D PLUGGED

For open soffits, built-ins, cable reels, walkways, separator boards and other interior or protected applications. Not a substitute for Underlayment or APA Rated Sturd-I-Floor as it lacks their puncture resistance. Touch-sanded. EXPOSURE DURABILITY CLASSIFICATIONS: Interior, Exposure 1. COMMON THICKNESSES: 3/8, 1/2, 19/32, 5/8, 23/32, 3/4.

(1) For nonstructural floor underlayment, or other applications requiring improved inner-ply construction, specify panels marked either "plugged inner plies" (also may be designated plugged crossbands under face or plugged crossbands or core); or "meets underlayment requirements."

(2) Also available in Underlayment A-C or Underlayment B-C grades, marked either "touch sanded" or "sanded face."

(3) Also may be designated APA Underlayment C-C Plugged.

(4) Underlayment and C-C Plugged panels 1/2" and thicker are designated by Span Rating rather than species group number in trademark.

Chart 3-22 continued.

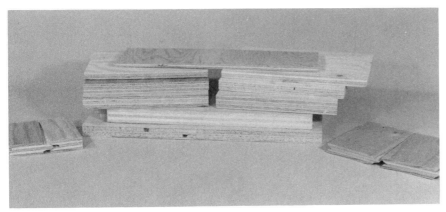

Illus. 3-190. Various types of plywood.

Bending Plywood

Bending plywood so that it can be used as an edging material (for example, to go around a tabletop) is not as difficult as it may seem. You can even make ¾-inch-thick plywood bend around a counter- or tabletop. Cut the edging to length, making sure that the top grain runs the length of the piece. Now, start making crosscuts in the edging strip, on 1-inch centers, the full length of the strip (Illus. 3-191). If you are using a table saw or a radial arm saw, make sure that the good side of the workpiece is up. Also make sure that the crosscuts extend to, but do not go into, the final ply of the wood. The spacing will vary with the radius of the curve that you require, so try this technique first on a scrap piece of material. Illus. 3-192 shows a 1½-inch finishing nail that I drove into the fence, just below the ½-inch mark, to help with the repeat cuts.

Carrying Plywood

I don't know just how much a 4 × 8-foot sheet of ¾-inch-thick plywood weighs, but it's difficult for an old guy like me to carry, so I came up with the carrying jig shown in Illus. 3-193.

Take a piece of ½-inch-thick plywood that is 12 inches wide. Put one end of it on the floor and lean it against your leg. Put your arm down and close your hand. Get someone to make a pencil mark on the plywood where your knuckles are. With your square, draw a line 3 inches below that mark. This will be the top of the handgrip, so the full length of the board will be a couple of inches above that. Cut out your handgrip.

On one side of the bottom, glue and screw two pieces of ¾-inch-thick plywood that are 2 × 12 inches. On the other side at the bottom glue and screw one piece that is also 2 inches wide by 12 inches long. On top of that piece place

Illus. 3-191. Make crosscuts in the edging strip the full length of the strip.

Illus. 3-192. The bent plywood.

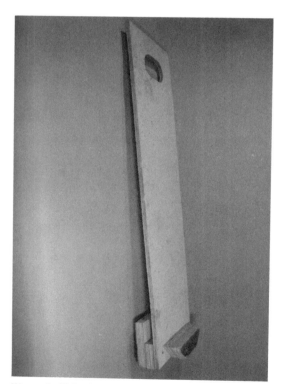

Illus. 3-193. A jig for carrying plywood.

another. Sand off the rough edges and you've got yourself a carrying jig.

On one side of the jig you can carry a ¾-inch-thick sheet of the plywood 3 inches wide × 12 inches long. On the other side, you can carry two ½-inch-thick sheets. Just make sure that the sheets are centered on the jig to make it balanced.

Adding Edging to Plywood

Here is a way to add edging to plywood. Let's assume, for example, that you want to add edging to a bookcase top that is 12 × 36 inches. Cut your piece 12¼ × 36¼ inches to compensate for a ⅛-inch saw kerf. Now, set your blade at a 45-degree angle and rip your top full length, making sure that you are cutting the full thickness (Illus. 3-194). Do the same thing to the ends. Save the off-cuts. Turn them over and glue them back on in their respective positions. You now have veneered edges on four sides (Illus. 3-195). A little practice on some scrap pieces will help.

Polystyrene, Description and Uses

Polystyrene is a white plastic material that is available in a wide range of thicknesses and is readily available from your local plastics dealer. This inexpensive material

Illus. 3-194. Set the blade at a 45-degree angle and rip your top full length.

Illus. 3-195. The plywood with veneered edging.

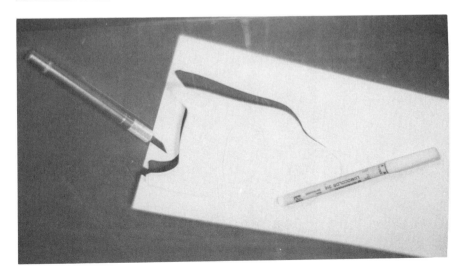

Illus. 3-196. Making a polystyrene pattern.

comes in a variety of sizes, but your dealer will usually cut to the size you want. I like to use polystyrene that is 1/64 or 1/32 inch thick. The thinner material can be cut with scissors, while the 1/32-inch material is more rigid.

Polystyrene is great for making patterns because it can be easily cut with a utility knife, scissors, band saw, or a stationary jigsaw. You can draw on it with a pencil or a soft-tip marker. Windex® glass cleaner will erase the pencil marks; the marker will probably be permanent.

To make a pattern, draw or trace it onto the polystyrene and then cut around the pattern lightly with a utility knife. Now, cut again, using a little more pressure. Bend the material and you will find that the pattern will start to separate from the sheet (Illus. 3-196). When the pattern is completely free, use a piece of fine sandpaper to smooth off the edges. Use the pattern. Then drill a hole near the top of it, mark it, and hang it up for future reference.

Portable Drill

(Also see Drill Press)

Unibit®

One of the best bits for drilling into materials such as sheetmetal, thin plastics, etc., is the Unibit® (Illus. 3-197). The Unibit is a stepped, tapered drill bit that comes in a variety of lengths, steps, tapers, and diameters. It is self-starting (it won't wander as do conventional bits), so it's ideal for portable drill use.

Stops

If you don't have any of the conventional screws on drill stops on hand to control the depth of your drill bit in your tool chest, try this technique: Wrap a piece of electrical or masking tape around the drill bit at the depth you want (Illus. 3-198). Drill slowly and carefully so that you can stop without tearing out the tape (Illus. 3-199).

Preventing Tear-Out

To prevent tear-out, or burring, when drilling through your workpiece, do the following: Place or clamp a piece of scrap wood under your stock and drill through your stock and into the scrap piece (Illus. 3-200 and 3-201). If you are using a sharp drill bit, this should prevent any chipping at the exit hole.

Illus. 3-197. The Unibit®.

Illus. 3-198. Masking tape is wrapped around the drill bit at the depth needed.

Illus. 3-199. Drilling into the wood.

Illus. 3-200. Drill through the stock into the scrap piece.

Illus. 3-201. The drilled hole.

Power Tools, Purchasing

The best way to find a power tool at less than full list price is usually through newspapers, ad flyers, store sales catalogues, flea markets, and friends. Be careful when shopping in stores for power tools. The advertised price from one store is not necessarily the best price. Shop around. Make sure the tool that you plan to buy will do what you expect it to. Do not sacrifice quality for price.

There are many imported tools that look like American or Canadian tools but are inferior in quality. Check their parts and the warranties carefully if you are considering buying them.

Project Planning

A pad of grid paper, available at your local stationery store, is a handy tool to have around the workshop (Illus. 3-202). The blue-lined squares are usually $\frac{1}{4} \times \frac{1}{4}$ inch, so it makes scaled drawing easy. Four squares across $\times$ eight squares up and down would represent a 4×8-foot sheet of plywood in $\frac{1}{4}$-inch scale. This is generally too small to work with in a workshop, so I use 1-inch scale (16×32 squares).

When building a bookcase, for example, draw it out on the pad and then draw out each piece of the cabinet separately. This will help you determine how much wood you need. You must remember, though, to take into consideration such things as the saw kerf (most saw kerfs are $\frac{1}{8}$ inch) and the grain direction.

You will find that by preplanning and laying out your project beforehand, you will not only save a lot of time, but you will save money as well by properly utilizing your wood.

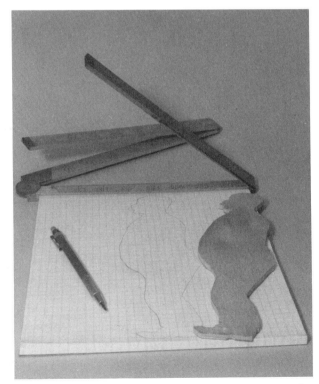

Illus. 3-202. Use grid paper to draw projects to scale.

Radial Arm Saw

Introduction to the Radial Arm Saw

I consider the radial arm saw the most important tool to have in a workshop. It's versatile and can be converted into a router, sander, drill press, shaper, planer, etc., in a relatively little amount of time (Illus. 3-203). Many tool catalogues display an array of accessories that can be used with the saw. Some of its detractors claim that the radial arm saw does not have the accuracy of a table saw. This might have been true 20 years ago, but today's radial arm saw is very accurate.

Angle Jigs

The angle jigs shown in Illus. 3-204 and 3-205 are made from ¾-inch-thick plywood scraps and are about 12 inches long. The holes in the top are used to hang the jigs on the pegboard, to keep them handy. They are easy and quick to make and really are timesavers when making quick cuts.

Illus. 3-203. The radial arm saw is a very versatile power tool.

Illus. 3-204. Using an angle jig.

Illus. 3-205. Keep a variety of angle jigs in your workshop.

Auxiliary Table

I built the extension table for my saw shown in Illus. 3-206 from a discarded countertop. It's connected to the saw table with an aluminum angle. The leg unit is from an old roller conveyer, but you can make a sawhorse type of leg or a hinged H-shaped leg. If you want to leave the extension table in place but be able to fold it down, use a piano hinge to fasten it to your saw table. The fence along the back is fastened with carriage bolts and wing nuts for easy removal. There definitely is an advantage to having a plastic laminate top. The stock being cut slides more easily. It should also be noted that the height of my table is the same as my workbench. This allows me to handle 10- or 12-foot-long materials.

Making Bowls

If you do not have a lathe, you can make a bowl with your radial arm saw (Illus. 3-207). This takes some practice and you have to cut a little at a time, but it's fun and it shows off the versatility of the saw. *Make sure that your work is secured.*

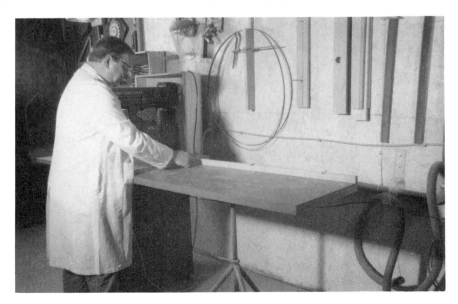

Illus. 3-206. A shop-made radial arm saw extension table.

Illus. 3-207. Making a bowl with a radial arm saw.

Cutting Circles

Making wheels or small, round tabletops on your radial arm saw is easy and fun (Illus. 3-208–3-210). First, make as many angle cuts as you safely can, to get your workpiece close to round. Place your workpiece on the saw table so that it will clear the back fence. If you want an 18-inch-diameter table, for example, the radius will be 9 inches. Therefore measure 9 inches from the edge of the extended blade and about 10 inches out from the fence. Drive a nail through the middle of the workpiece and into the saw table (Illus. 3-208). Make sure it rotates freely. Now, holding the stock securely at the extreme left of the blade, start cutting a little bit at a time. **Note:** *Do not attempt this procedure unless you are very familiar with the tool.*

Corner Mitring

One of the easiest ways of doing a series of mitre cuts for picture frames, etc., is to use a Sears Craftsman mitre jig on your radial arm saw (Illus. 3-211 and 3-212). This eliminates the need to continually swing the arm for successive cuts and makes measuring much easier because the jig has built-in stops. Using this jig gives you a longer reach with the saw. And, with the built-in stops, you don't have to remeasure when you flip the workpiece over.

Crosscutting with a Radial Arm Saw

Most woodworkers have found themselves in this type of situation. You have approximately a dozen pieces of ¼-

Illus. 3-208. Driving a nail through the middle of the workpiece and into the saw table.

Illus. 3-209 and 3-210. Cutting the circle.

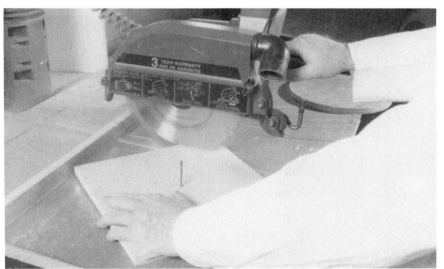

Illus. 3-210. Cutting the circle.

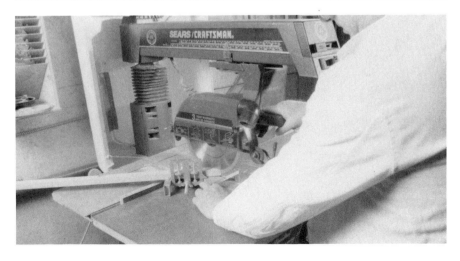

Illus. 3-211 and 3-212. Using the Sears Craftsman mitre jig.

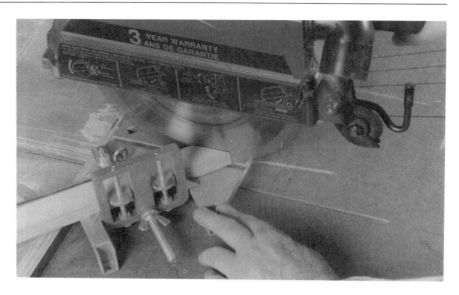

Illus. 3-212.

inch-thick plywood to crosscut. The stock that you have is off-cuts that are all 12¾ inches wide. Your radial arm will cleanly crosscut 12 inches of stock. Normally, then, you would have to flip the piece over and cut it again. This would mean two operations.

To eliminate the need to make two cuts, place a piece of 1 × 2 or 1 × 4 under your workpiece, close to the front of the saw table (Illus. 3-213). Clamp it down or use double-face tape to hold it securely. The workpiece will now be sloped towards the fence. This ¾-inch rise at the front should be high enough to put the blade through the stock to make a complete cut. If not, try a thicker piece of scrap or move the scrap closer to the fence.

Extension Roller

I built the inexpensive extension roller shown in Illus. 3-214 and 3-215 out of scrap wood and an old typewriter roller. I made its height adjustable so I can use it with my router table and my band saw. To save time trying to find the proper height for the roller, I marked the holes on the roller according to the type of tools I use with it. I later modified the roller by installing a T nut and a hex bolt through the holes to give me infinite heights. The roller works well for handling long pieces of stock at the in-feed end of the saw.

Extra Fences

Radial arm saw fences always get cut up, especially after you have made a lot of compound-angle cuts and dadoes. Make two or three spare ones out of ¾-inch plywood (Illus. 3-216). Drill a hole in the ends of them and hang them up where they are handy.

A higher, longer fence is sometimes desirable, especially when you are doing a lot of ripping (Illus. 3-217). I

Illus. 3-213. Placing a piece of wood under the workpiece makes it easier to crosscut pieces that are normally too wide to be cut in one cut.

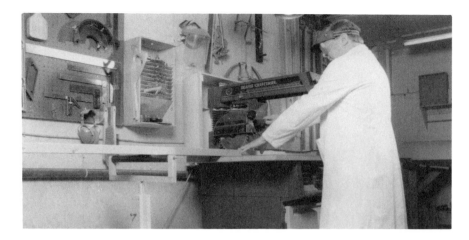

Illus. 3-214. A shop-made extension roller for the radial arm saw.

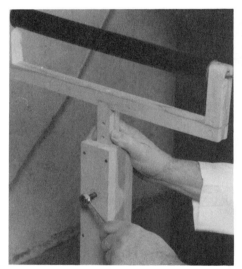

Illus. 3-215 (above left). The T nut and hex bolt make the extension roller easy to adjust to the proper height.
Illus. 3-216 (above right). Make extra fences for the radial arm saw. They will prove handy.

Illus. 3-217. A longer shop-made fence for the radial arm saw.

use a piece of hardwood 2½ inches wide × 6 feet long. I find this fence particularly helpful when ripping a sheet of plywood by myself. Drill a small hole in its end and hang it up close to your saw.

Mitre Cuts

When mitred crosscuts are made with the saw arm in a 90-degree position, there is a tendency for the workpiece to slide into the saw blade. Following are two ways to help prevent this from happening to you:

The first method consists of placing a couple of pieces of double-face tape on the underside of your workpiece (Illus. 3-218). Make sure, though, that this doesn't change the levelness of the work.

The second method is to stick a piece of sandpaper along the fence near the cut, using double-face tape, and another piece farther along the fence to ensure a square cut (Illus. 3-219).

Panel-raising

As shown in Illus. 3-220, panel-raising with a radial arm saw can be done quite easily with the use of an auxiliary table attachment. Set your blade horizontally, adjust it to the desired cut angle, and feed your workpiece through slowly.

Push Stick

Illus. 3-221 shows a push stick that I always use with a radial arm saw. It looks like a backsaw with the blade removed. When making it, make sure the "blade" part of the push stick is long enough to push your stock all the way through without jeopardizing your hands.

Illus. 3-218. Adding double-face tape on the underside of your workpiece will make it easier to make mitre crosscuts with the radial arm saw.

Illus. 3-219. Another way to make mitre crosscuts with a radial arm saw is to stick a piece of sandpaper along the fence near the cut with double-face tape, and another piece farther along the fence.

Illus. 3-220. This auxiliary table attachment makes it easy to panel-raise with the radial arm saw.

Storing the Push Stick

I was constantly misplacing my radial arm saw push stick until I came up with the following idea: I stapled a strip of Velcro® to the side of it and stapled the hook portion of the Velcro to the side of my blade cabinet, which is right next to my saw (Illus. 3-222). The black Velcro strip on the push stick serves as a reminder to me to put it away.

Repetitive Cuts with the Radial Arm Saw

Method #1

The simplest way to make repetitive cuts of the same length is to clamp a piece of scrap wood to the fence at the distance from the blade for your particular needs (Illus. 3-223). Be certain that the scrap is tightly clamped.

Illus. 3-221 (above left). Push stick. **Illus. 3-222 (above right).** The Velcro® on the side of this push stick allows it to be stored on the side of the blade cabinet.

Illus. 3-223. A simple way of making repetitive cuts of the same length with a radial arm saw.

Method #2

A method that I like to use for making repeated crosscuts is shown in Illus. 3-224 and 3-225. This auxiliary fence is made from an old laminated countertop made from high-density particleboard. Cut the fence to the desired length and height. The fence in Illus. 3-225 is about 1 inch higher than usual. Place it in position and secure it. Then make a saw cut through it with the radial arm saw set at 0, and draw a pencil line full length where the saw table meets the fence.

Now, measure exactly ⅝ inch from both edges of the kerf and precisely every ⅝ inch thereafter, to both ends of the fence. This will give you ½-inch centers.

Set up your drill press with a ¼-inch bit, set your rip fence on the table, and adjust it so that when you start drilling into the new saw fence the holes will be just slightly above the penciled line that you drew. Try this on some scrap first. Start drilling your holes all the way through the new saw fence, on half-inch centers, the entire length of the fence.

Now, add the stop pin. For this, you can use ¼-inch dowelling or, as I have, a ¼-inch steel rod.

To complete the fence, mark the top of it to indicate the full inches. Drill one more hole in the end of it and hang it up near your saw.

Illus. 3-224. This auxiliary fence is being used to make crosscuts.

Illus. 3-225. Using the auxiliary fence.

Method #3

Next time you want to make repeated kerfs such as you would make in plywood for the purpose of making a table edge (see Plywood, Bending), try this timesaving technique: Assuming that you are making ½-inch cuts, drill a ⅛-inch hole ½ inch from the saw kerf on your fence. Drill it ¼ inch above the table surface, and drill it all the way through. Put the fence back into position, put a snug-fitting common nail through the hole from the back side, and this jig is now ready to be used (Illus. 3-226).

Make your first cut with the workpiece against the nail.

Slide the piece over so that the kerf of that cut slips under the nail, and repeat the cut.

Method #4

The jig shown in Illus. 3-227 and 3-228 is very helpful for making repeat cuts without having to remove the fence. Scraps of ¾-inch-thick plywood are all that is required. Before assembly, however, install a T nut in the back. The appropriate-size hex bolt will serve to tighten it against the fence.

Illus. 3-226. Using a shop-made jig to make crosscuts.

Illus. 3-227. This jig is very helpful when you are crosscutting with a radial arm saw.

Illus. 3-228. Note the T nut on the back of the jig.

Method #5

Imagine the following: A club has asked you to make 150 backing boards for some small plaques which they will honor their members with. The backing boards are $\frac{1}{2} \times 2 \times 10$ inches. You have already ripped your stock to 10 inches. Now you have 149 crosscuts to make. Here's a technique to help you make these crosscuts: Set your stop block (see method #4) 2 inches out from the blade, but put a scrap piece of $\frac{1}{2}$-inch stock under it (Illus. 3-229). Now, tighten the bolt.

Next, place a piece of plywood $\frac{1}{4}$ inch or thinner on the table, tight to the fence and to the right of the blade. This piece should be long enough to hold your workpiece flat.

Now, make your first cut (Illus. 3-230). After your cut is complete, the cut piece will drop down and, as you slide the uncut portion to the left, the cut piece will slide under the block and eventually into a box placed beside the saw.

Ripping Thin Strips

Here is a shortcut to *safely* rip long, thin strips (approximately $\frac{1}{4}$ inch wide $\times$ $\frac{3}{4}$ inch thick) on the radial arm saw. Glue and screw two pieces of $\frac{3}{4}$-inch-thick plywood together. The bottom piece should be 3 inches wide $\times$ 3 feet long, and the top piece should be 4 inches wide $\times$ 3 feet long. Drill a $1\frac{1}{2}$-inch-diameter hole through the two thicknesses, about 3 inches in from the ends, depending on the length of your fence. The holes are to accommodate the spring clamps that are used to clamp the jig to the fence. The jig is now complete. Clamp it in place, turn your blade to the rip position, and lock it $3\frac{1}{4}$ inches out from the fence. Turn on the saw and lower it through the jig and to the table surface (Illus. 3-231). This will produce $\frac{1}{4}$-inch strips.

I drilled a small hole just in front (not too close) of

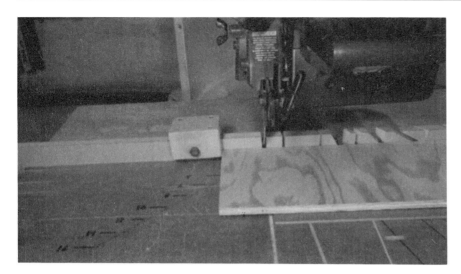

Illus. 3-229. Set your stop block two inches from the blade and put a piece of ½-inch stock under it.

Illus. 3-230. Making a cross-cut.

Illus. 3-231. The saw has been lowered though the jig and onto the table surface.

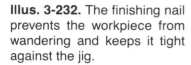

Illus. 3-232. The finishing nail prevents the workpiece from wandering and keeps it tight against the jig.

where the blade enters the jig and put a 1½-inch finishing nail in it to prevent the strip from wandering and to keep it tight against the jig (Illus. 3-232).

Roller Table Extension

The extension shown in Illus. 3-233 allows me to handle 4 × 8-foot sheets for ripping on my radial arm saw. It is made of rollers salvaged from an old, discarded roller conveyer. I place it slightly over a foot from the front of my saw table. This allows me to squeeze in between the saw and the extension table to adjust and turn the saw on/off. When I use the extension table and my front roller stand, I am able to rip a ¾-inch sheet of plywood without any assistance.

Sanding

There is no need to buy an expensive sanding disc for your radial arm saw. You can make one (Illus. 3-234 and 3-235). Simply cut a piece of ⅜-inch plywood into a 10-inch-diameter circle and drill a hole into the center of the circle equal in size to your arbor. Sand the disc smooth and apply a couple of coats of polyurethane to both sides. Make sure, of course, that the arbor hole is dead center.

Apply adhesive-backed sanding discs to your shopmade disc. These discs are available at most hardware stores. Apply discs of different grit to each side. An alternate method is to apply rubber cement to a sandpaper sheet and the disc and adhere the sheet to the disc. You may have to patch in a spot, but if the joint is tight, this

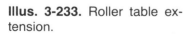

Illus. 3-233. Roller table extension.

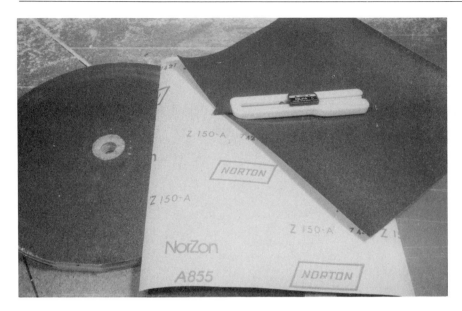

Illus. 3-234. The materials and tools needed to make a sanding disc.

Illus. 3-235. The shop-made sanding disc.

won't matter. The sheets are less expensive than the adhesive discs.

Finally, mount the disc on the radial arm saw using the arbor washers, and bolt it down tight.

Setting the Fence on a Radial Arm Saw

Some radial arm saws have thumbscrews that are used to tighten the table sections to the fence. Here is a method that offers an alternate approach to tightening the table sections with thumbscrews: Use a 2½-inch hole saw to make wheels out of ¾-inch plywood scraps. Next, drill out slots in the middle of the wheels with a bit that is slightly smaller than the thickness of the thumbscrews. Then sand the wheels and force-fit them over the screws (Illus. 3-236). Be careful when tightening. Do not apply too much torque or you will break off the support bracket.

Shop-made Tabletop Surfaces

Method #1

Save wear and tear to your saw's tabletop by adding an extra top (Illus. 3-237). Cut several pieces of ³⁄₁₆-inch wall

Illus. 3-236 (above left). The wheels fit over the screws and make it easier to tighten the table sections to the fence. **Illus. 3-237 (above right).** The materials and tools needed to make a tabletop surface.

panelling to size. (Wall panelling is the type of panelling with printed wood grain on one side.) Put all but one aside. These are spares. Vacuum off your saw table and run three or four lengths of double-face tape along the length of the table. Run a strip across the table on both sides of where the saw kerf should be, but don't overlap the tape. Place the new surface paper-pattern-side down and tap it down with a piece of scrap and a mallet. Use a palm sander to smooth it off (Illus. 3-238).

You might want to cut some pieces for the back sections as well, and tape them down.

Method #2

I discovered another way to make a tabletop for my radial arm saw: with off-cuts of tempered hardboard (Masonite®) left over from a job that I did. One advantage of using Masonite is that it is smooth. But because Masonite tends to cup, I had to use a few more nails in it to make sure it stayed flat. I was careful, though, to make sure that the ⅝-inch common nails were placed away from the blade's path. I purposely used common nails so that their heads would be seen in the event that I mistakenly placed them in the blade's path, but made sure that their heads were nailed flush.

Illus. 3-238. Use a palm sander to smooth the tabletop.

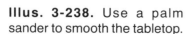

Next, I decided to print angles directly on the tabletop with my adjustable drafting angle to the right of the saw blade. To the left of the blade, I drew a diagonal line (45 degrees) and began to mark the spots for nailing when I wanted to make wheels or discs. I punched a mark every two inches with my awl and marked these as diameters, 2, 4, 6 inches, etc. (Illus. 3-239).

While you are cutting one top, you might as well cut two or three and put the spares away for future use. It will save you from having to remeasure later.

Tape Measure Fence

Here is a helpful technique that I learned some time ago:

Take one of your spare saw fences, set it in place on your table, and make a 90-degree crosscut through it. Remove it and run a strip of double-face tape down the length of it near the top. Take a cloth measuring tape and stick it to the fence. Cut it off at the end (Illus. 3-240). The cut-off piece can usually be turned over so that you can stick it on the other portion of the fence. However, one side will probably be upside down.

This should save a lot of measuring time when you are doing crosscuts. Just be sure, though, that the same type of blade is used and that the fence is properly aligned.

Illus. 3-239. The completed tabletop.

Illus. 3-240. Making a tape measure fence.

Taper Ripping

There are a number of ways to rip a piece of stock to make tapers. By far the easiest is to use the Sears Craftsman taper jig (Illus. 3-241 and 3-242). This tool eliminates the need to figure angles and make jigs when ripping tapers. It comes with a full set of instructions.

Cutting Crooked Lumber

Method #1
Lumber will sometimes warp (become crooked) laterally along the grain, and will lose its straight edge. Normal

Illus. 3-241 and 3-242. Using the Sears Craftsman taper jig to make tapers.

Illus. 3-243 (right). An easy method for ripping crooked lumber.

methods of cutting don't work in this situation and you generally either discard the piece or let it collect dust on your wood rack.

Try this method for ripping crooked lumber straight: Nail a 2 × 2-inch piece (or similar stock, as long as it is straight) to the length of your board along one edge (Illus. 3-243). Set your saw to the rip position. Lock the carriage. Now, run the board through the saw, with the 2 × 2 at the edge of the board and tight against the fence of the saw and the extension tables.

Method #2

Here's another easy technique for ripping crooked lumber. Take a piece of aluminum or steel angle (1 × 1-inch or larger), and screw it to the top edge along the length of your board. The length of the aluminum angle should exceed the length of your stock (Illus. 3-244). The overhang of the aluminum should now run along the outer edge of your radial arm saw table. Set your saw to rip and proceed to cut the inner edge. Remove the aluminum angle, reset your saw, and rip that side.

Worn-out Fence

When you think that your fence is worn out due to excessive cuts, don't throw it in the scrap bin. Instead, remove it and turn it over (Illus. 3-245). If the fence was not too high, you will be able to use it again. To check, make a crosscut where the old slot was. If it cuts completely through the fence, then the fence cannot be used.

Illus. 3-244. Another method for ripping crooked lumber.

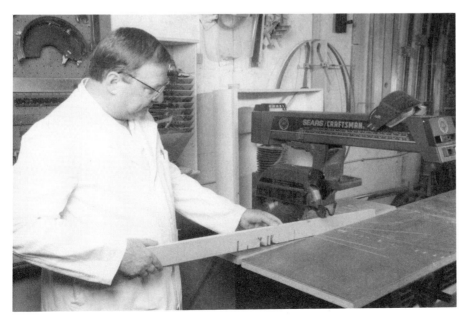

Illus. 3-245. If the fence has become worn, turn it over.

Rafter Angles

Random Orbital Sanders

Chart 3-23 and Illus. 3-246 will eliminate the need to calculate angles when making rafters. This will be very helpful when you are building that backyard shed or even that dream house.

Random orbital sanders are very popular tools. The circular disc on the machine rotates, but in a random fashion, so

RISE PER FOOT	ROOF PITCH	ANGLE OF CUT
4 inches	1/6	18½ degrees
6 inches	1/4	26½ degrees
8 inches	1/3	33¾ degrees
9 inches	3/8	37 degrees
10 inches	5/12	39¾ degrees
12 inches	1/2	45 degrees
14 inches	7/12	49½ degrees
15 inches	5/8	51¼ degrees
16 inches	2/3	53 degrees
18 inches	3/4	56¼ degrees
20 inches	5/6	59 degrees
24 inches	FULL	63½ degrees

Chart 3-23.

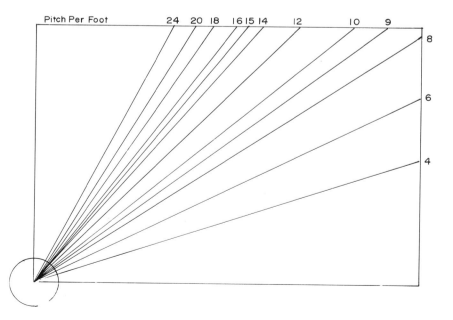

STANDARD RAFTERS

Illus. 3-246. Standard rafter angles.

the tool is very effective as a finishing sander. With a 180- or 220-grit paper disc and the sander set on top speed, you get a silky-smooth finish. An added advantage is that it does not leave any swirls or gouges. The machine is very light and is much quieter than most of the belt sanders that I've used.

There are two types of random orbital sanders. One is a right-angle sander that is quite large and similar to a grinder. The smaller machine, as shown in Illus. 3-247, works like a palm sander. It revolves at 12,000 opm (orbits per minute). It has a unique hard, porous plastic dust receptacle that doubles as a vacuum attachment. It is also very quiet.

Illus. 3-248. Random orbital sanders will accept adhesive-backed discs.

Illus. 3-247. A random orbital palm sander.

Both machines accept the adhesive-backed discs (Illus. 3-248). The disadvantage of using adhesive-backed discs is that when you change discs of different grits, you don't know what to do with the used one. In most cases, it won't stick back on because of sawdust, fingerprints, etc. The Teflon® backing sheet won't adhere properly, either.

There is a product now available that eliminates this problem. Both machines offer a pad that will accept a Velcro®-backed sanding disc. This product is sometimes referred to by manufacturers as a hook-and-loop sanding disc. It takes very little time to change this disc. Dust and small chips do not stick to it. Other advantages to the hook-and-loop disc are that it will accept products like Bear-Tex® and will work like a polisher when a piece of felt is adhered to it.

Router

Accessories for the Router

There are many accessories available that can be used. The router is an extremely versatile tool. Chart 3-24 describes accessories sold by Sears. There are also many books on router use available on the market that will prove helpful.

Auxiliary Base

Using your existing base as a template, make two or three spare router bases out of ⅛-inch-thick clear Plexiglas® (Illus. 3-249). Make the center hole of the bases slightly larger than your biggest bit. Round off the outer edges with a piece of fine sandpaper. A clear base makes free-hand routing a lot easier because you can see much more of the surface that you are working on.

Leave the protective paper on the spare bases until you are ready to use them. Do not store the bases where direct sunlight will come into contact with them.

Compass Base

With a piece of ⅛-inch-thick Plexiglas®, make a compass

TOOL	USE
Bowl crafter	For making various sizes and styles of bowls
Dovetail jig	For making dovetail furniture joints
Edge crafter	For making round or elliptical picture frames or tabletops
Lathe	For making table or chair legs, as well as spiral-cutting
Pantograph	For duplicating, enlarging, or reducing patterns, as well as for lettering
Signmaker	A set of lettering templates for making signs
Table	An accessory that turns the router into a jointer and makes edge-shaping easy

Chart 3-24.

Illus. 3-249 (above left). This router base has been made out of ⅛-inch-thick clear Plexiglas. **Illus. 3-250 (above right).** This compass base has been made from ⅛-inch-thick Plexiglas.

base for your router (Illus. 3-250). Copy the base that comes with the router, but add a 12-inch pan handle on one side. Find the middle of the handle and drill ¹⁄₁₆-inch holes down it, spacing them every ¼ or ½ inch. Spacing the holes each ¼ inch will give them more versatility.

Set your router on your workpiece with the new base on it and tap a finishing nail through the desired hole.

Moulding Jigs

Making small, shaped mouldings is easy if you make and use the moulding jig shown in Illus. 3-251. Clamp the jig securely to your router table and feed your workpiece slowly through the opening.

Measuring Your Router's Cutting Radius

Measure the distance from the center of your router collet to the outer edge of your router base plate. Write this distance with a soft-tip marker on a sticky label and adhere it to the motor housing for future reference (Illus. 3-252). This will save repeated measurements later.

Push Pads

The router or planer push pads shown in Illus. 3-253 are made from scraps of pine. The bases and the handles are ¾ inch thick. Make the basic shape of the handles on your band saw or scroll saw, and the final fit with your drum sander. The pads under the bases are of foam rubber. I used pipe insulation and put it on with double-face tape.

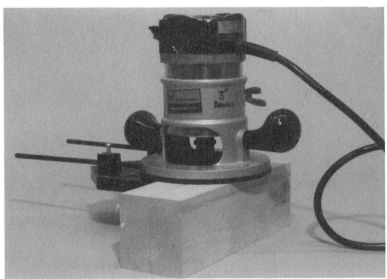

Illus. 3-251. The plywood clamped against the workpiece will prevent the workpiece from wandering when its edge is being shaped or routed.

Illus. 3-252 (above left). Note that the router's cutting radius is written on the label adhered to the motor housing.
Illus. 3-253 (above right). Shop-made push pads.

Router Bits

Cleaning

As with saw blades and drill bits, router bits also need cleaning. Gum and tar will build up on the bits after use and will aid in the dulling process.

Soak the bits in a mixture of washing soda and water until you can remove the gum with a stiff brush (Illus. 3-254). A toothbrush will work well. When they are clean and dry, spray them with some silicone (Illus. 255). This will help delay any further buildup.

Router bits can also be cleaned with oven cleaner (Illus. 3-256). Spray it on, let it stand for a few hours and then wipe it off. Rinse the bit in warm water, dry it, and then spray it with silicone.

Illus. 3-254. Removing gum and tar from a bit with a toothbrush.

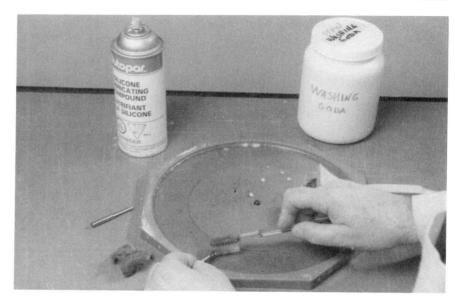

Illus. 3-255. When the bit is clean and dry, spray it with some silicone.

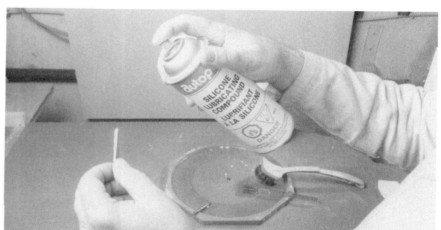

Illus. 3-256. Cleaning the bit with oven cleaner.

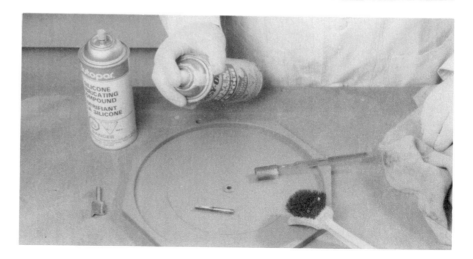

Storing Router Bits

I was told many years ago to *never* leave a tool with a blade in it, blade-down, on a workbench. Since then, I have always bought or built a holder or case for all my blades and bits.

The router-bit holder shown in Illus. 3-257 is very easy to make. Space the holes far enough apart to prevent the bits from touching one another.

Testing Bits

Always test your router bits out on a piece of scrap before using them on your workpiece (Illus. 3-258). Make several cuts with the bit set at various heights in the router, to determine whether the appearance of the finished project will be acceptable.

Rubber Cement, Description and Uses

Rubber cement (sometimes called paper cement) is an excellent temporary adhesive for use around the workshop (Illus. 3-259). I use it when stacking several pieces of stock together for multiple-pattern cutting. The cement won't leave a deep stain on the wood and can be rubbed off with your finger. A little gentle prodding with a putty knife will separate the pieces.

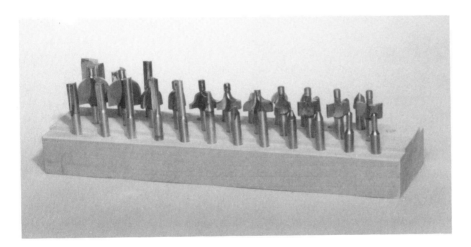

Illus. 3-257. Router bit holder.

Illus. 3-258. Testing a router bit.

Illus. 3-259. Rubber cement.

Rubber cement is applied in much the same way as contact cement in that you coat both sides, let them stand for a minute or two, and then join the pieces together. It's not necessary to completely cover the surfaces; a few dabs in the corners will probably suffice for temporary adhesion.

Rubber cement can be purchased in varying quantities at most art-supply stores.

Rust Check®

Rust Check® is a rust-inhibiting, oil-like substance that is usually used on automobiles but works equally well on tools. There is usually a Rust Check dealer in every town and city, so obtaining the product will not pose a problem.

Somewhere in your workshop is a container full of rusty nuts, bolts, and screws, and probably a screwdriver as well. Now's your chance to make use of them. Take an old windshield washer fluid container and cut a rectangular piece out of one side. Leave the cap on. Dump the rusted parts in it and then pour either paint thinner or engine cleaner on them. Let them sit for a couple of days and then drain the paint thinner or engine cleaner and wipe the parts. Dry them off, clean out the container, put the parts back in, and pour Rust Check over them (Illus. 3-260). After a day or so, drain but don't discard the Rust Check. The used Rust Check can be used again for a few more applications.

Use Rust Check on such things as band-saw tables, table or circular saw tables, plane and planer bases, or any other metal surface that may have a tendency to rust. Simply wipe it on generously, let it sit overnight, and then wipe it off. Spills can be cleaned up with dishwasher liquid and water.

Illus. 3-260. These screws, nuts, and bolts have been cleaned with Rust Check.

Safety Glasses

Importance of Safety Glasses

There is no point to keeping your safety glasses tucked away in a drawer, because chances are you will forget to use them. Hang them from your busiest power tool (Illus. 3-261). I keep mine on the arm of my radial arm saw, so it's pretty hard not to see and use them.

Keep a few extra pairs of safety goggles around the shop. They will come in handy when visitors are working with you. Don't allow anyone near your tools without goggles or a safety visor on. Don't go near a tool without wearing some form of eye protection.

Types of Safety Glasses

The finest safety glasses that I've ever seen are the ones shown in the top left of Illus. 3-262. They are made by Miniman® of Sweden and can be bought at most tool-supply stores. The advantage of these safety glasses is that they not only protect the eyes, but the forehead and temples as well. The glasses flip up or down out of the visor portion, and there is a stop on them so that they don't smack the bridge of your nose when they are flipped down. They are made to fit over regular glasses. The real advantage to using these glasses is that you can wear them all the time you are in your shop because they are very comfortable.

I taped an extra, flexible lens over my glasses to extend their life. For two dollars, your local plastics dealer will sell you some thin, flexible Lexan. This can be cut with scissors to make a set or two of spare lenses (Illus. 3-263).

This is not to say, however, that these are the only good safety glasses around. Any safety glasses are excellent if they are government-approved. Norton® Canada makes a good set of safety glasses that have wide stems on them for added protection.

Illus. 3-261. These safety glasses are stored on top of the radial arm saw.

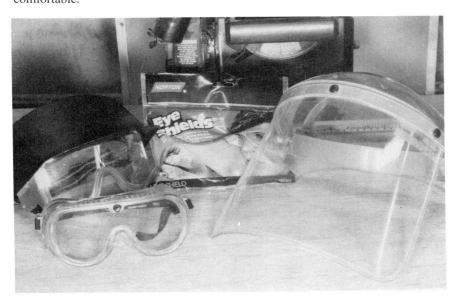

Illus. 3-262. Note the different types of safety goggles.

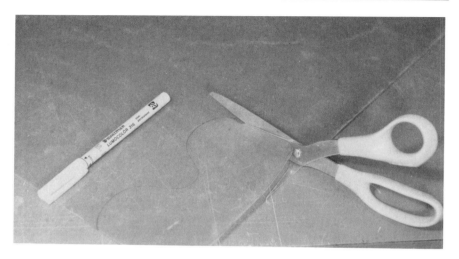

Illus. 3-263. Lexan can be used to make spare lenses for safety glasses.

Controlling Sawdust Buildup

Most safety glasses are made of plastic, and plastic attracts sawdust. Many times, I have put on a safety shield covered in sawdust, only to think that maybe somebody turned off the lights.

To help minimize sawdust buildup on your safety glasses, wipe them occasionally with a used sheet of fabric softener (Illus. 3-264). It will help stop static cling.

Sanders

(See Belt Sander, Drum Sander, and Random Orbital Sanders)

Sanding Belts

Extending the Life of Sanding Belts

To extend the life of your sanding belts at least tenfold, purchase a crepe block from your woodworking supply catalogue (Illus. 3-265). They only cost about $5.00, and they are very economical. I bought two of them about two years ago and I still haven't used the second one.

After you have used your sander, with the sander on, apply the crepe block with some pressure to the belt. It will "erase" all or most of the residue that has built up on the belt. Be sure to do this after every time you use the sander.

You can also use the crepe block on your sanding drums, discs, and even on your orbital sander.

Illus. 3-264. One way to control sawdust buildup on safety glasses is to wipe them occasionally with a used sheet of fabric softener.

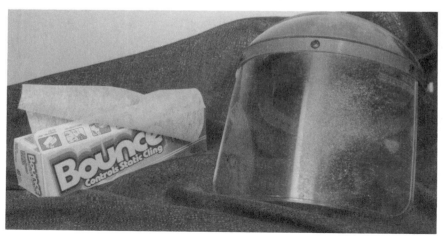

Illus. 3-265. A crepe block can be used to remove all of the residue that has built up on the sanding belt.

Sanding Techniques

Sanding Concave Surfaces

Hand-sanding concave surfaces can be difficult because it is hard to maintain the flat shape of the edge with your finger wrapped in sandpaper, as one would normally do. Try this shortcut the next time: Take a piece of dowel as close as possible in diameter to what you want to sand. Wrap a piece of sandpaper around it, grit side out, and leave a "tail" at each end so that they may be clamped together. Close the plates of an old butt hinge over the tails and tighten it with a small bolt and wing nut (Illus. 3-267).

Sanding Small Parts

There are times when you have to use your stationary belt sander to clean a small part. These little parts have a tendency to slip between the fence and the sanding belt. To prevent this, clamp a piece of ¼-inch-thick plywood that is as wide as the belt to the sander's fence. Clamp it so that it is snug against the sanding belt (Illus. 3-268). Then, carefully proceed to sand your small workpiece (Illus. 3-269). The additional fence will prevent your workpiece from sliding under the metal fence.

Storing Sanding Belts

Throwing your sanding belts into a drawer haphazardly will shorten their lives. If you take care of them and store them properly they will last for a long time. I screwed a number of dowels to a pegboard on which to drape belts of different sizes and grits (Illus. 3-266). Be sure the dowel length is at least equal to the belt width.

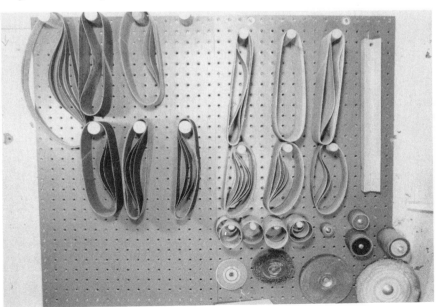

Illus. 3-266. This is an excellent storage method for sanding belts.

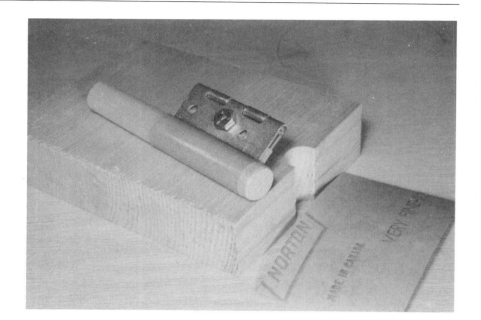

Illus. 3-267. This shop-made aid can be used to sand concave surfaces.

Illus. 3-268 (above left). A piece of plywood is clamped right against the sander's fence. **Illus. 3-269 (above right).** Sanding the small workpiece.

Sandpaper

(See Abrasives)

Saw, Circular

(See Circular Saw, Radial Arm Saw, and Table Saw)

Sawhorses

Most workshops do not have the room for two regular-size sawhorses. Illus. 3-270 shows a folding sawhorse made from 1 × 4-inch stock with a piano hinge along the top edge. The chains near the bottom limit it's opening distance. Two of these sawhorses hanging on a wall take up less than 4 inches in depth.

Another sawhorse is shown in Illus. 3-271. The main frame is 36 inches high × 72 inches long. The two hinged extensions are 36 inches long. When opened up, they will hold a full sheet of plywood or similar panel-type material, to make cutting easier.

The advantages of this type of sawhorse is that it folds away flat and replaces *two* regular sawhorses that are usually cumbersome to handle and difficult to store.

Illus. 3-270. A portable sawhorse.

Illus. 3-271. Another type of portable sawhorse.

Scrapers, Honing

A quick and easy way to hone your scraper is the method shown in Illus. 3-272, using your stationary belt sander. Do this in short bursts, though, because you don't want to destroy the temper in the blade.

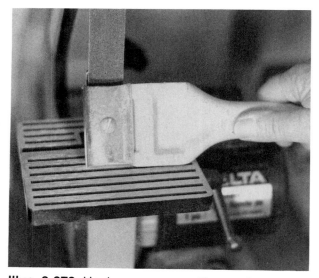

Illus. 3-272. Honing a scraper with a stationary belt sander.

Scratch Awl

(See Awl)

Screws

Wood Screws

Wood screws are comprised of a head and a shank, with most or all of the shank being threaded. Wood screws come in a variety of different shapes (Illus. 3-273 and 3-274). Each one is designed for a specific purpose. These shapes range from flat head to round head to pan head to bugle head. Most screws come in lengths starting at ¼ inch and go up to 6 inches or more. The diameter of the screw is called the gauge and is usually expressed in whole numbers, e.g., #7 × 1¼ inches long.

The drive of the screw can vary as well, as can be seen in Illus. 3-274. The Robertson®, or square-drive, screw is very popular in Canada and is becoming popular in the United States. This is my personal favorite because the drive will take more torque than a slot drive. Another

Illus. 3-273. A sample of the variety of available screws.

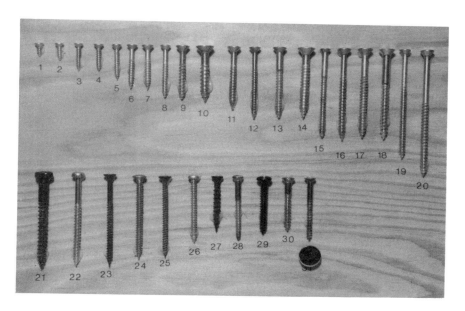

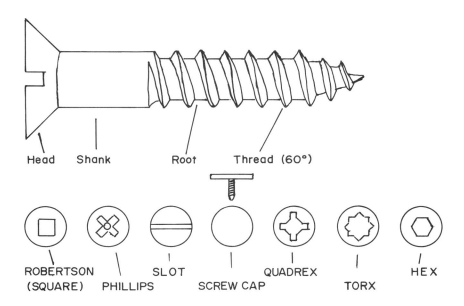

Head   Shank   Root   Thread (60°)

Illus. 3-274. Anatomy and shapes of screws.

ROBERTSON   SLOT   QUADREX   HEX
(SQUARE)   PHILLIPS   SCREW CAP   TORX

advantage is that a Robertson screwdriver will hold the screw so that you can reach those difficult corners. The Quadrex® screw will accept both a Robertson and a Phillips® screwdriver. The slot-drive screw is becoming obsolete.

The bugle-head screw (also known as a drywall screw) is now regularly used in woodworking, especially for fastening plywood and other softwoods. These screws are often available in the Phillips drive, but I have seen them in square drives as well. The advantage is that they do not require a pilot hole. When using them, though, make sure that the two pieces of stock are held tightly together before screwing, because there is no unthreaded shank to pull the pieces together. Another advantage is that the drywall screw is self-countersinking.

Broken Screws

When a screw breaks off just as you are assembling your finally completed project, you count to ten, curse anyway, and then take your portable drill and carefully drill a 1/16-inch hole on an angle through the edge of the wood and into the screw. Do this a couple of more times in different positions. Now, use a pair of needle-nosed pliers to grip and remove the screw remains (Illus. 3-275).

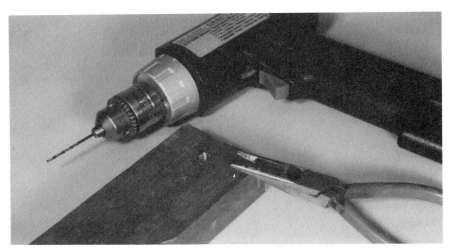

Illus. 3-275. Using a pair of pliers to remove the screw remains.

The next step is to repair the hole. Drill a hole slightly larger than the existing one by using a bit that is equal in size to a dowel that you have on hand (Illus. 3-276). Cut the dowel to its proper length and glue and insert it into the hole, making sure that the grain in the dowel runs in the same direction as your workpiece. Select a screw larger in gauge than the one removed, drill a new pilot hole, and countersink and carefully drive the screw home.

Countersink Covers

Try this technique for making countersink covers: Buy a common paper-hole punch from a stationery store. This tool is great for punching out "dots" in veneer (Illus. 3-277).

Put a little contact cement on the screw head and the veneer, and you have a perfect screw cover.

Illus. 3-276. Drill a hole slightly larger than the existing one.

Illus. 3-277. A paper-hole punch can be used to punch out dots in veneer.

Pocket Jig for Screws

When pocket screws are required, as in the assembly of furniture, the jig shown in Illus. 3-278 will save you a lot of time and frustration. Drill down the middle of a piece of 1 × 1-inch hardwood stock that is about 3 inches long using a ⅜-inch bit. Now, determine the angle for the pocket screws (usually 15 degrees), set your saw accordingly, and cut about an inch off the bored stock.

Next, glue it to the larger piece so that it makes a squared bottom as shown in Illus. 3-278. Cut a little off the bottom if necessary, to adjust the point of entry. Clamp the jig to your work and drill the pocket with a ⅜-inch bit. Once done, remove the jig and drill your pilot hole.

This jig may take a little bit of time to put together, but if you make furniture, it will save a lot of time later.

Purchasing Screws

The next time you are in your local hardware store to pick up some screws for your project, buy square-drive screws, also known as Robertson screws. These screws have a square hole in their tops and will take more torque than the conventional slot- or Phillips®-head screws (Illus. 3-279). Another advantage is that the screwdriver will actually hold the screw so it can be placed in vertical or overhead positions. These screws cost about the same as the other types of screws.

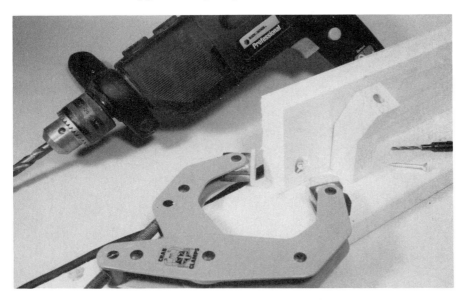

Illus. 3-273. Pocket jig.

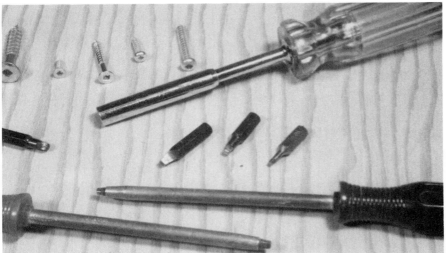

Illus. 3-279. Examples of square-drive screws.

Scroll Saw

Extending Blade Use

Only about one-third of your scroll-saw blade gets used, so to extend the life of the blade, try the following technique: Cut out a piece of ¾-inch-thick plywood that is as large as the table on your saw, sand it, and finish it with a couple of coats of polyurethane (Illus. 3-280). Now, when you think your blade is getting dull, stick this new tabletop on top of the regular one, using double-face tape, and you'll end up using the top portion of your blade, which will still be sharp.

Cutting Thin Material

Material ⅛, ³⁄₁₆, or ¼ inch thick is sometimes difficult to saw on a stationary scroll saw because it tends to ride with the blade. To solve this problem, attach a scrap piece of ½-inch-thick material to your workpiece with dabs of rubber cement or double-face tape. An alternate technique is to attach several more pieces of the same stock as your workpiece. This will make the workpiece easier to control (Illus. 3-281 and 3-282).

After your pattern is cut out, do not remove the ½-inch scrap. Keep it on because the workpiece will be easier to handle when sanded with a power sander. If you want to duplicate the pattern at a later date, mark the scrap piece appropriately and store it in a safe place.

Illus. 3-280. This table placed on top of the tabletop will extend the blade life of scroll-saw blades.

Illus. 3-281. The scrap piece attached to the workpiece makes it easier to cut the thin material.

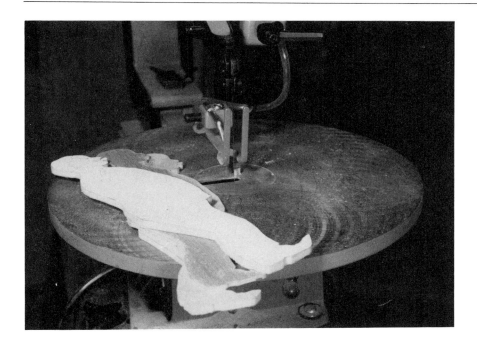

Illus. 3-282.

Shaper Blades

Cleaning Shaper Blades

Arm and Hammer® washing soda mixed with water in a shallow plastic container is an efficient way to clean your shaper blades of tar and resin buildup. Soak them in the solution for approximately 10 minutes and use an old toothbrush or a copper wire brush to scrub them clean (Illus. 3-283). Wipe them dry and spray them with silicone (Illus. 3-284). Store them in their original plastic containers.

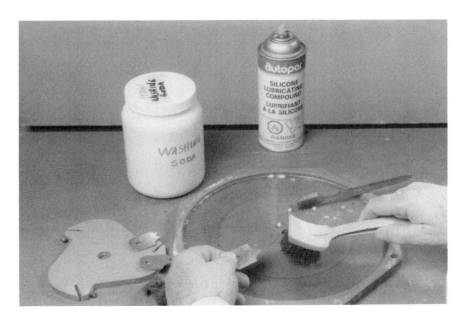

Illus. 3-283. Use an old toothbrush or a copper wire brush to remove tar and resin from the shaper blade.

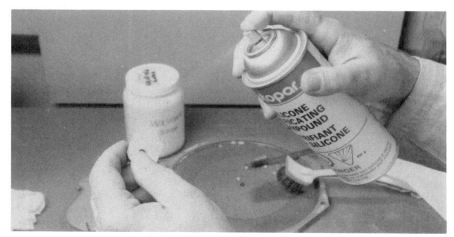

Illus. 3-284. The shaper blade is being sprayed with silicone.

Sharpening Shaper Blades

An easy way to sharpen your shaper blades is to lay them flat-side down on an oilstone and rub them back and forth (Illus. 3-285). Make sure, however, that the stone's surface is flat. This can be checked with a square. After sharpening them, put them back into their plastic cases and add a few drops of Rust Check. Wipe them dry before using them, and then give them a squirt of silicone spray.

Shaper Head

Description and Uses

The shaper head is also referred to as a moulding head or cutter head. Sears sells a Craftsman shaper head that is very effective and reasonably priced for the home work-shopper. The head itself is a heavy disc that fits on the arbor of your saw. On the disc are three slots in which the shaper blades are locked into position with Allen screws. The blades can only fit one way, so there is little chance of making a mistake; but still be careful.

A special table insert has to be used for a table saw. An adjustable blade guard for a radial arm saw is required, unless you are using it in a crosscut situation, in which case the regular blade guard should be used.

There are about 20 different blade sets available that will cut an almost infinite number of patterns. These sets can be used to make tongue and grooves, coves, beads, sashes, ogees, glue joints, flutes, etc. Setting your shaper head to different angles will vary the patterns as well.

Illus. 3-285. Sharpening a shaper blade on an oilstone.

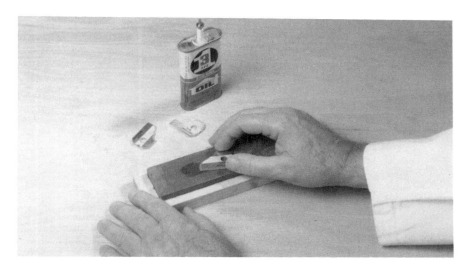

Crosscutting with a Shaper Head

The initial cut with a shaper head in a crosscut position on your radial arm saw will produce a splintered edge. There are two ways to prevent this from damaging your workpiece. First, make your workpiece about 2 inches wider than necessary and cut it to size later. Second, put a 2-inch piece of scrap of the same thickness between the fence and your workpiece (Illus. 3-286).

Slabs, Making

A slab, in woodworking terminology, is a broad surface of wood, hard or soft. As an example, a solid-core interior door is called a slab door.

The most common way of building a slab-top table is to glue a number of narrow strips of wood together, side by side, until the desired width is obtained, and then clamp them together (Illus. 3-287). When the glue has set, plane or sand both top and bottom surfaces and then, if desired, veneer both sides.

The advantage of using narrow strips is that they can be cut from a wider board and reassembled with their grain direction alternated. Now, should an individual board warp, it would be restrained by the boards adjacent to it. It is highly unlikely that the entire slab would warp or distort if properly glued up.

If you plan to veneer the slab, make sure that you veneer *both* sides so that the tension created by the drying of the glue will be equalized.

Illus. 3-286. The scrap piece between the fence and the workpiece prevents the shaper head from damaging your workpiece.

Illus. 3-287. A slab-top table.

Spade Bits

(See Drill Bits)

Staining

(See Wood Stain)

Steel Wool

(See Abrasives)

Styrofoam,® Cutting

Professionals cut Styrofoam® with a hot-wire cutter that gives the edges a moulded look. This method isn't practical for those working in workshops. Here are alternative methods: For thicker pieces, use a fine-toothed hacksaw or fretsaw blade and support the material so that you can hold both ends of the blade while cutting. Cut thinner material with a razor-sharp, double-sided Styrofoam knife (Illus. 3-288). Whichever method you use, keep a vacuum handy to pick up the crumbs.

Tables, Auxiliary

(See Type of Tool Being Used)

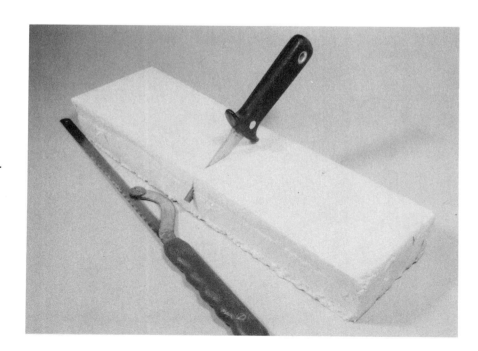

Illus. 3-288. Two methods for cutting Styrofoam®.

Table Saw

(Also see Radial Arm Saw)

Table Saw Accessories

Chart 3-25 lists some of the accessories available for your table saw that will make your tool more versatile.

Adjusting a Table-saw Mitre Gauge

Here are two shortcuts for truing up your table-saw mitre gauge. In the first method, turn the gauge upside down and put it in the gauge slot at the edge of the table. If you note any light between the edge and the gauge, as indicated in Illus. 3-289, adjust the gauge.

In the second method, put your mitre gauge in the left-hand slot and place a builder's square along the front with the tail lined up with the right-hand slot (Illus. 3-290). Adjust the mitre gauge if required.

ACCESSORY	DESCRIPTION
Blade Stabilizer	Blade stabilizers are made of aluminum. They help prevent any wobble on a 10- or 12-inch saw blade
Dado Blade	Dado blades are available either in sets or as an adjustable wobble blade
Hold-Down Jig	Hold-down jigs attach to your mitre gauge to help prevent mitre cuts from riding up
Sanding Disc	Sanding discs are available in 10- or 12-inch sizes with adhesive-backed aluminum-oxide paper
Shaper Head	When coupled with the various blades available, shaper heads can be used to make mouldings, etc
Table Insert	Table inserts are available in various sizes for dado blades and shaper heads
Taper Jig	Taper jigs help in making tapered cuts accurately
Universal Jig	Universal jigs hold your stock to edge or end dadoes safely and accurately

Chart 3-25. A list of some of the accessories available for the table saw.

Illus. 3-289 (above left). The light shining on this mitre gauge indicates that it has to be adjusted. **Illus. 3-290 (above right).** Use a builder's square to adjust the mitre gauge.

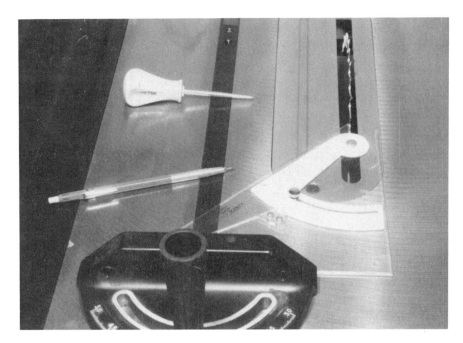

Illus. 3-291. To ensure accuracy when cutting 45-degree angles, measure the angle with a draftsman's adjustable square, and then scribe a line on the table saw across the mitre slots.

Ensuring Accurate Angles

To ensure accuracy every time you cut a 45-degree angle on your table saw and to make sure your mitre gauge is always accurate, measure the angle with a draftsman adjustable angle, and then scribe or draw a line on your saw table across the mitre slots (Illus. 3-291).

Ensuring Fine Angles

To ensure that you are cutting precisely at 22½ degrees or other fine angles, purchase an adjustable square from your local art-supply store (Illus. 3-292). This will be useful for checking angles on drawings as well.

Cleaning the Table

Keep your saw table clean and slick by giving it a regular cleaning. Dust off the table (and other parts of the saw as well) and apply a generous amount of Rust Check to the surface. Let it stand overnight and then wipe it off. Now, spray some silicone on the surface and wipe it off (Illus. 3-293).

Extension Roller (See Radial Arm Saw)

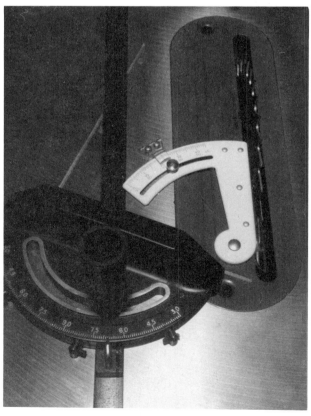

Illus. 3-292. Use an adjustable square when cutting at fine angles.

Taper Ripping (See Band Saw and Radial Arm Saw)

Tape, Types and Uses

Following is a description of the variety of tape available (Illus. 3-294):

Double-face tape is available in a paper or cloth base and in widths of ¼ to 6 inches or more. A roll or two of ½-inch paper tape is handy to have around the shop for use as a temporary tacking material, such as when stacking a number of pieces of wood for multiple pattern cutting. The surfaces should be clean and dry.

Duct tape is a cloth, colored adhesive tape that is very strong and can be used for a multitude of temporary repairs. It is available in widths from ½ to 3 inches or more.

Electrical tape is black vinyl tape that usually comes in rolls that are ½ or ¾ inch wide. It is always useful around the shop for temporary wire repairs. This tape also comes in a variety of colors, so it may be used for tool identification or, if stapled to the ends of boards, for wood identification, e.g., red for oak, blue for teak, etc.

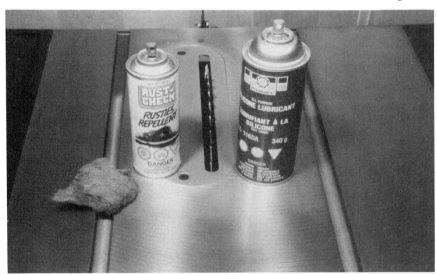

Illus. 3-293. To keep your table clean, apply Rust Check to the surface, let it stand overnight, and wipe it off. Then spray silicone on the surface and wipe it off.

Illus. 3-294. Tape is available in many different types.

Masking tape is usually used to cover sections of an area that is being painted, but can be used for many tasks in the workshop. It is available in various widths. I've found ½-inch-wide masking tape to be the most practical to have around the shop.

Removing Adhesive Tape

When attempting to remove adhesive tape that has been stuck to an object for a while, you are usually left with a gummy residue. A squirt or two of WD-40® will usually melt the adhesive so that it may be wiped off with an old rag (Illus. 3-295).

Masking tape that has been on for a while will usually lift off quite readily after you have warmed it up with a hair drier.

Templates, Enlarging

To enlarge a template or pattern of, for example, a circle or an ellipse by ½ inch all around, simply place a washer of the appropriate size against the template, place your pencil point in the center of the washer, and run it around the pattern (Illus. 3-296).

Tenons, Making Round

Place a piece of square stock (e.g., 2 × 2 inches) into a 2-inch-diameter plastic or cardboard tube so that it fits snugly. Leave enough of the stock protruding for the length of the tenon desired, and brace the tube against the radial arm saw fence (Illus. 3-297) or the mitre gauge for a table saw. Set your blade to the required height and start your cuts (Illus. 3-298). Do not rotate the tube while cutting.

Illus. 3-295. To remove adhesive from wood, squirt it with WD-40® and wipe it off with a rag.

Illus. 3-296. Enlarging the pattern for a circle.

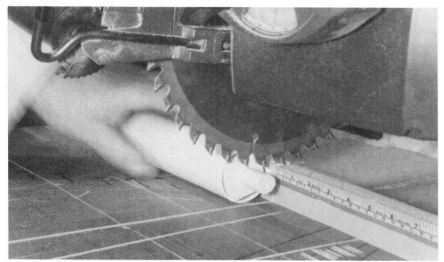

Illus. 3-297. Bracing the tube against the radial arm saw fence.

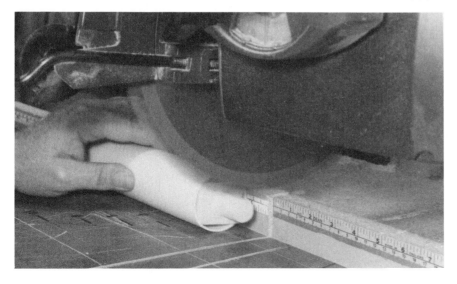

Illus. 3-298. Cutting a round tenon. Do not rotate the tube while cutting.

Thickness Planer, Planing Small Pieces

Sometimes workpieces are just too small to safely place in a thickness planer. Here is a safe way of handling small workpieces: Spot-glue or nail two long strips of wood of the same thickness as your workpiece to its sides to form an H. Slowly feed this H-shaped jig through the planer, and then remove the scraps (Illus. 3-299).

Tools, Securing

Although this information is given in Chapter 2, it is worth repeating. The best way of keeping your portable power tools safe and out of reach of children or the inexperienced is, of course, to lock up your workshop or keep your tools locked in a cabinet. Sometimes, though, this isn't convenient.

If you have to leave your tools out or your shop unlocked, buy some inexpensive, small padlocks like the one shown in Illus. 3-300. Insert the hasp through the plug prong holes and lock them. You may be able to lock up three or four tools with one padlock. If the prong holes are too small, drill them to size.

Illus. 3-299. Feeding a small piece through a thickness planer.

Illus. 3-300. Small padlocks can be used to lock up your power tools.

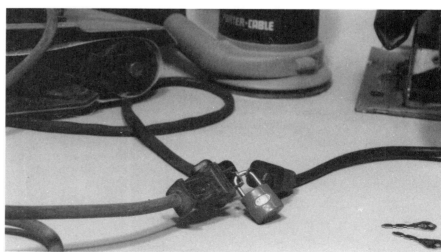

Toothbrushes, Cleaning Tools with

Believe it or not, you can find a use for your old toothbrush in your workshop. Keep it in your tool box or drawer. It will come in handy for cleaning your saw blades and router

and drill bits, and for applying paint remover to those intricate details on your latest refinishing project (Illus. 3-301).

Veneer

Characteristics of Veneer

The Random House dictionary defines veneer as a thin

Illus. 3-301. Old toothbrushes can be used to clean saw blades, router and drill bits, and even to apply paint remover to a refinishing project.

Illus. 3-302. Veneer.

Different Veneer Cuts Produce Different Patterns

1. **ROTARY CUTTING** peels the veneer into long sheets, much like unwinding a roll of paper. The result: a wide and variegated grain pattern.

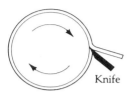 

2. **PLAIN (FLAT) SLICING** through a half-log produces a light variegated grain similar to that of sawn lumber.

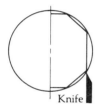 

3. **HALF-ROUND SLICED** is cut from a rotated half-log to produce a veneer with the character of both rotary and plain-sliced.

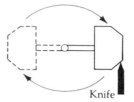 

4. **RIFT-CUT** veneer is produced from a quarter log and shows an accentuated vertical grain.

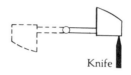 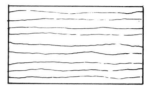

Veneer Matching Can Produce Beautiful Effects

1. **BOOK MATCHING** — Every other sheet of a flitch, which is a sequence of veneers peeled or sliced from the same log, is turned over, like the pages in a book.

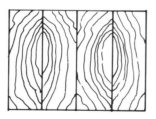

2. **SLIP MATCHING** — Every sheet of the flitch is joined side-by-side, without turning the figure. Normally specified when even colour is desired and on straighter grained veneers.

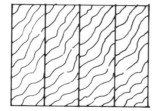

3. **UNMATCHED** — Veneers are assembled with no particular grain pattern.

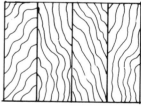

4. **WHOLE PIECE FACE** — The panel face comprises a single sheet of veneer, with a continuous grain character across the complete panel.

Illus. 3-303. Veneer. (Courtesy of Canadian Hardwood Plywood Association)

layer of fine wood used to cover a cheaper, thicker wood. This definition is somewhat simplistic.

Veneer is a very thin (1/64 inch or so) panel of wood that is shaved off a log with a very sharp knife (Illus. 3-302 and 3-303). The panels are called flitches. These flitches vary in width and thickness depending on the type of cut and the type of wood that they are cut from. A wood like pine, for example, is soft and relatively pliable and can be cut very thin, whereas oak is harder and more brittle and must be cut thicker.

The width of the flitches depends on the diameter of the tree and the type of cut. *Rotary-cut veneer* will be wider because the knife slices off a thin layer while the log is being rotated. *Flat-cut veneer* is narrower because the knife slices off a flat section of the log. *Rift*, more commonly known as *quarter cut*, is produced from a log that has been cut in quarters lengthwise. *Half-round veneer* is produced in the same manner as quarter-cut veneer. These four methods of producing veneer result in four dramatically different effects in the grain figuring.

Types of Veneer

The following is a brief description of most of the veneers that are available in the United States and Canada.

African mahogany is imported from West Africa. It ranges in color from light pink to reddish brown. The wood produces a very pleasing and distinct grain. The trees are found up to 4 feet in diameter with heights of up to 70 feet clear of limbs, so very wide veneer flitches may be had. Mahogany is used almost exclusively in boat-building and furniture-making.

African rosewood, also known as bubinga, akume, and kewazinga, is imported from West Africa. Red, with streaks of dark purple, this highly figured wood is in much demand for rich, dark furniture and as wall panelling in formal dens and libraries. African rosewood is not a true rosewood.

American cherry grows in the eastern half of North America. Primarily used for furniture, its light-red to light-brown natural color is preferred by the connoisseur, even though it accepts stains quite readily. It is elegantly figured.

American elm grows in the American Midwest. It is a heavy, hard, strong, and very coarse-grained wood that is light brown in color.

Avodire is imported from the Gold and Ivory coasts of Africa. It is one of the main "blond" cabinet woods. It ranges in color from cream to pale yellow and is moderately figured.

Brazilian rosewood is a true rosewood. True rosewood,

as known to cabinetmakers, comes from Brazil, Central America, Asia, and the Malagasy Republic. It has excellent technical properties, an attractive appearance, and is usually quite fragrant. The wood is fairly easy to work and finishes to a smooth, high polish that holds well over a long period of time. Another asset is that it is dimensionally stable. Unfortunately, almost all of the mature trees have been used up and thus it is very expensive. The smaller trees are now being harvested and used mainly for flat-cut veneer.

Butternut is wood from the Northeast United States. It is a pale, satiny brown with a leafy grain and occasional dark streaks. It is used mainly in furniture because it ages beautifully and takes on a mellow patina.

East Indian rosewood, also known as Bombay rosewood, is imported from Sri Lanka and southern India. It ranges in color from dark purple to ebony and has streaks of red or yellow. When the veneer is cut on the quarter, it is dramatically figured.

English brown oak is white oak that has been turned brown by a harmless fungus. If harvested healthy, the wood is like white oak, but if it has been pruned or damaged, the fungus will develop in the tree. The result is a rich-brown color. The density and the highly figured grain make it particularly desired for furniture-making.

Figured red gum, also known as sweet gum, grows in the moist lands of the lower Ohio and Mississippi basins. The heartwood of the gum tree, it has a reddish-brown tone. It is used mostly for cabinetry.

Lacewood, sometimes referred to as Australian silky oak, is imported from Australia. Its flaky grain pattern turns a pinkish-red when finished.

Limba, also sold as Korina in the United States, has a grain of medium texture and hardness and good woodworking properties. A graceful, delicate figure is exposed when this wood is finished.

Macassar ebony is imported from the West Indies. The logs vary in size up to 16 inches, with some reaching 30 inches. It ranges in color from dark brown to black with streaks of golden yellow. It is a very dense and heavy wood and is considered quite rare.

Makori is a Nigerian wood that is also called African cherry, baku, and cherry mahogany. Makori is dense and hard and ranges in color from pinkish- to blood red. It is similar to closed-grained mahogany.

Maple is noted for its beautiful colors in the autumn months. Found throughout the northeastern United States and eastern Canada, this hard, strong, closed-grained tree is used for furniture because of its color, which ranges from cream to light brown. The sugar maple is used primarily for the production of syrups and sugar products.

Mountain tulip, more commonly referred to as yellow poplar, is a large tree found from Canada to the Gulf of Mexico. A greenish-yellow wood with dark streaks, it is a great surface for stains and paints. Tulip is used in furniture construction such as drawer parts.

Oak grows in the entire eastern United States and Canada. White oak is slightly lighter than red oak, but, when finished, they are hard to tell apart. The properties of the wood make it particularly suitable for watertight containers.

Orientalwood is imported from Australia. It is somewhat similar to American walnut in both color and grain, but is not related. The tree is huge, often reaching heights of 190 feet with a diameter of 6 feet. As a veneer, it is usually cut on the quarter to produce a strong stripe-like effect.

Paldao, a native of the Philippines, is a large tree with a base of 3–4 feet. The wood is fairly hard with large pores and is grey to reddish-brown with irregular stripes and a varied grain. Used for architectural woodwork and furniture, paldao finishes very well.

Pine is most prevalent on the East and West coasts of North America. It is a softwood that is used in construction, furniture, panelling, and for a myriad of other products. As a veneer, it is cut very thin because it is very pliable and soft. As a result, veneered surfaces should only be lightly sanded before finishing.

Primavera is a Central American tree that has a cream-to-yellow-brown color and a mahogany-like grain that makes it particularly suitable for furniture and fine cabinet work. When finished, it has a high-golden satin luster.

Red birch is grown in the eastern United States and Canada. It is the heartwood of the birch tree and is reddish-brown in color. The wood is heavy, hard, and closed-grained and is one of the principal woods used to produce wood alcohol, charcoal, tar, and oils. Stained, it is sometimes used to simulate other, more expensive woods.

Sapele is a reddish-brown wood that is grown in Ghana and Nigeria. It has a very strong stripe and is reminiscent of African mahogany, but is harder and heavier. Fine cabinetmakers make good use of this beautiful wood.

Satinwood originates in southern India and Sri Lanka. It is a pale-gold wood that is nearly always found with a rippled figure and a prominent straight stripe. The wood is hard and dense with an interlocking grain.

Teak is a rare wood that originates in Burma, East India, and Southeast Asia. It is very expensive. The sap in this wood is left to drain for about five years before the tree is cut down, and the sap leaves an oily substance in the pores that makes the wood highly water-resistant. It varies in color from golden yellow to dark brown, and usually has dark streaks in it. Teak is much in demand by boat builders. The oil in the wood and its density make it very hard on woodworking tools.

Tigerwood, or Congowood, is a West African wood. It ranges in color from greyish-brown to gold with black markings, and has an excellent ribbon effect. These characteristics make tigerwood a desired wood for cabinetmakers.

Walnut, better known as American black walnut, is found generally throughout the southeastern United States. It ranges in color from light grey to greyish-brown to dark-purplish-brown. The figured effect as seen in some veneers is a result of the half-round slicing. Some other interesting veneers are sliced from the stump, crotch, and burls.

White ash is a large tree found mainly in eastern Canada and the United States. It is a tough, heavy wood that is used for baseball bats and the bent parts of furniture. It ranges in color from a creamy white to a dark brown and sometimes has a red tinge to it. Its pattern is prominent and is used for rustic effects.

White birch is from the same tree as red birch, but it is the sapwood. It has little or no grain pattern and is usually found only in flat-cut veneers.

Zebrawood originates in the African Cameroon and Gaboon West Africa. It is a wood with highly contrasting stripes that is very heavy and hard and is often used as inlay. The stripes alternate from a straw yellow to a dark brown.

Applying Veneers

A quick and easy way to apply veneer to *small*, flat workpieces is to use adhesive fabric (Illus. 3-304). This is available at most fabric shops. Simply lay it between the veneer and your stock, place a piece of brown paper on top, and use a hot, dry iron to press it all in place.

Make sure, though, that the *center* of the iron face covers all of the edges.

Cutting Veneers

Wood veneer is much too thin to cut on a power saw, but sometimes this has to be done. Here is a shortcut: Sandwich the veneer between a couple of scrap pieces of ⅛- or ¼-inch plywood using double-face tape to adhere them (Illus. 3-305). Draw your pattern on the top surface and proceed to saw. Carefully separate the pieces when they are completed.

Gluing Veneers

Gluing veneers is a slow process if you are gluing both sides of the workpiece, unless you have a commercial veneering press. You have to glue one side of the veneer and then one side of your workpiece, let them dry, and then repeat the process for the other side. The following shortcut will help expedite the gluing process: Tap a 1-inch finishing nail into each corner of your workpiece and apply your contact cement to this side. Flip it over so that it is resting on the nails and glue this side (Illus. 3-306). Glue up your veneer pieces. When they are tacky and ready to apply, adhere them to the top surface, flip it over, remove the nails, and do that side. Apply your clamps.

Repairing Veneers

Occasionally a bubble will appear on a piece that you have recently veneered. Most likely, this is due to an absence of glue beneath that spot, or the glue in that spot was too dry to adhere. If the latter is true, apply some heat to the area with a hair dryer or heat gun. Be careful not to burn it; get it just hot enough so that you can still touch it. Now, place a heavy weight on top of the area to compress the bubble onto the heated surface. Let it stand for a few hours. If this doesn't work, it's because there was no glue to adhere to, so try the following technique: Your doctor or your phar-

macist will give or sell you a hypodermic needle, after you explain what it is for. Get one that is fairly large, large enough to allow white or carpenter's glue to pass through with some pressure. Put a few drops of the glue into the syringe and inject it into the bubble. Clamp the spot down. The bubble will disappear (Illus. 3-307). Rinse the syringe out thoroughly in warm water, replace the safety cap, and *lock it away* for future use.

Waferboard

(See Particleboard)

Wall Brackets, Making

Here's a dandy idea for hanging those tool cabinets on the

Illus. 3-304. Use adhesive fabric to apply veneer to small, flat workpieces.

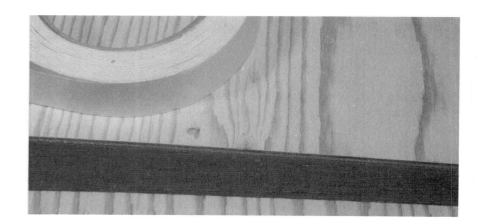

Illus. 3-305. Use double-face tape to adhere scrap pieces to veneer.

Illus. 3-306. Gluing veneers.

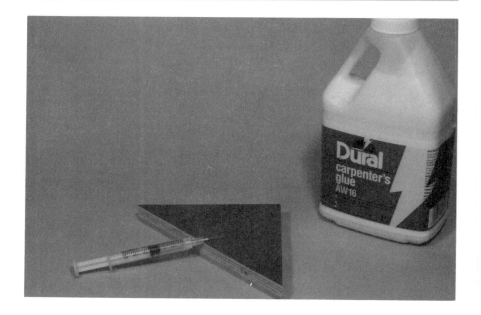

Illus. 3-307. To eliminate a bubble on veneer, inject a few drops of carpenter's glue into the bubble.

wall of your workshop. It's not only easy, it's fast. Rip a 45-degree cut in a couple of 1 × 2's, full length. Cut two pieces to size, the width of your cabinet. Glue and screw them to the back of the cabinet at the top and the bottom as shown in Illus. 3-308. Cut two or more pieces the same length and screw one piece to the wall, where you want the top of the cabinet to be. Hang the cabinet and mark where the bottom bracket should be. Remove the cabinet, secure the bottom rail, and rehang the cabinet.

Save the leftover pieces. Once you see how easy it was to make these brackets, you'll find more cabinets to hang this way.

Wire Wheels, Extending the Lives of

After a wire wheel has been used to remove rust or paint, the wires seem to all be running in the same direction and the wheel tends to lose its effectiveness. Extend the life of the wheel. After every use, remove it from the arbor and reverse it (Illus. 3-309 and 3-310). You'll probably double its life.

Wood

(See Hardboard, Hardwood, Lumber, Particleboard, and Plywood)

Wood Stain, Oil, Applying

Instead of using a paintbrush to apply wood stain, which you will have to clean afterwards, use scraps of foam rubber or pieces of an old sponge (Illus. 3-311). When you are done, just throw them away.

Workbench, Light for

To add more light to your workbench, do the following:

Illus. 3-308. Wall brackets.

Illus. 3-309 and 3-310. To extend the life of a wire wheel, remove it from the arbor and reverse it.

Illus. 3-311. Use foam rubber or an old sponge to apply wood stain.

Illus. 3-312. Lighting for the workbench.

Install a drapery I-beam track above and running the length of your workbench. Run a lamp wire through the roller loops, attach a lamp socket and shade on one end and a plug on the other, and gently squeeze the loops so that they grab the wire (Illus. 3-312). Be careful: Don't break the outer cover of the wire.

Workbench Dogs, Using

Workbench vise dogs can sometimes mar a workpiece. To help prevent this from happening, cover the ends of the dogs with neoprene tubing (available at your plastics dealer) or other resilient material such as foam rubber, Styrofoam® packing, flat wood scraps, etc. (Illus. 3-313).

Workmate®

The Black & Decker Workmate® is a very versatile tool, and no workshop should be without one (Illus. 3-314). It serves as a mini workbench, a large clamp, and as an extra pair of hands.

The Workmate does have limitations, though. One limitation is its reach. One way to extend its reach is to use the extensions shown in Illus. 3-315.

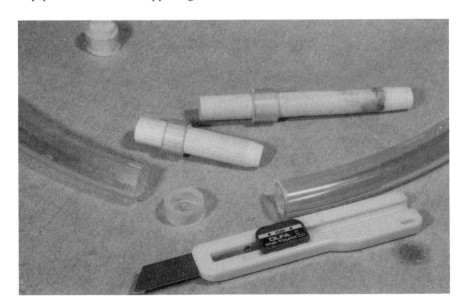

Illus. 3-313. To prevent dogs from marring a workpiece, cover the ends of them with neoprene tubing or other resilient material.

Illus. 3-314. The Black & Decker Workmate will prove very valuable in the workshop.

Illus. 3-315. The four extensions on the Workmate lengthen its bite.

Appendices

WEIGHTS AND MEASURES

Unit	Abbreviation	Equivalents In Other Units of Same System	Metric Equivalent
Weight			
		Avoirdupois	
ton			
short ton		20 short hundredweight, 2000 pounds	0.907 metric tons
long ton		20 long hundredweight, 2240 pounds	1.016 metric tons
hundredweight	cwt		
short hundredweight		100 pounds, 0.05 short tons	45.359 kilograms
long hundredweight		112 pounds, 0.05 long tons	50.802 kilograms
pound	lb *or* lb av *also* #	16 ounces, 7000 grains	0.453 kilograms
ounce	oz *or* oz av	16 drams, 437.5 grains	28.349 grams
dram	dr *or* dr av	27.343 grains, 0.0625 ounces	1.771 grams
grain	gr	0.036 drams, 0.002285 ounces	0.0648 grams
		Troy	
pound	lb t	12 ounces, 240 pennyweight, 5760 grains	0.373 kilograms
ounce	oz t	20 pennyweight, 480 grains	31.103 grams
pennyweight	dwt *also* pwt	24 grains, 0.05 ounces	1.555 grams
grain	gr	0.042 pennyweight, 0.002083 ounces	0.0648 grams
		Apothecaries'	
pound	lb ap	12 ounces, 5760 grains	0.373 kilograms
ounce	oz ap	8 drams, 480 grains	31.103 grams
dram	dr ap	3 scruples, 60 grains	3.887 grams
scruple	s ap	20 grains, 0.333 drams	1.295 grams
grain	gr	0.05 scruples, 0.002083 ounces, 0.0166 drams	0.0648 grams
Capacity			
		U.S. Liquid Measure	
gallon	gal	4 quarts (2.31 cubic inches)	3.785 litres
quart	qt	2 pints (57.75 cubic inches)	0.946 litres
pint	pt	4 gills (28.875 cubic inches)	0.473 litres
gill	gi	4 fluidounces (7.218 cubic inches)	118.291 millilitres
fluidounce	fl oz	8 fluidrams (1.804 cubic inches)	29.573 millilitres
fluidram	fl dr	60 minims (0.225 cubic inches)	3.696 millilitres
minim	min	1/60 fluidram (0.003759 cubic inches)	0.061610 millilitres
		U.S. Dry Measure	
bushel	bu	4 pecks (2150.42 cubic inches)	35.238 litres
peck	pk	8 quarts (537.605 cubic inches)	8.809 litres
quart	qt	2 pints (67.200 cubic inches)	1.101 litres
pint	pt	½ quart (33.600 cubic inches)	0.550 litres
		British Imperial Liquid and Dry Measure	
bushel	bu	4 pecks (2219.36 cubic inches)	0.036 cubic metres
peck	pk	2 gallons (554.84 cubic inches)	0.009 cubic metres
gallon	gal	4 quarts (277.420 cubic inches)	4.545 litres
quart	qt	2 pints (69.355 cubic inches)	1.136 litres
pint	pt	4 gills (34.678 cubic inches)	568.26 cubic centimetres
gill	gi	5 fluidounces (8.669 cubic inches)	142.066 cubic centimetres
fluidounce	fl oz	8 fluidrams (1.7339 cubic inches)	28.416 cubic centimetres
fluidram	fl dr	60 minims (0.216734 cubic inches)	3.5516 cubic centimetres
minim	min	1/60 fluidram (0.003612 cubic inches)	0.059194 cubic centimetres
Length			
mile	mi	5280 feet, 320 rods, 1760 yards	1.609 kilometres
rod	rd	5.50 yards, 16.5 feet	5.029 metres
yard	yd	3 feet, 36 inches	0.914 metres
foot	ft *or* '	12 inches, 0.333 yards	30.480 centimetres
inch	in *or* "	0.083 feet, 0.027 yards	2.540 centimetres
Area			
square mile	sq mi *or* m²	640 acres, 102,400 square rods	2.590 square kilometres
acre		4840 square yards, 43,560 square feet	0.405 hectares, 4047 square metres
square rod	sq rd *or* rd²	30.25 square yards, 0.006 acres	25.293 square metres
square yard	sq yd *or* yd²	1296 square inches, 9 square feet	0.836 square metres
square foot	sq ft *or* ft²	144 square inches, 0.111 square yards	0.093 square metres
square inch	sq in *or* in²	0.007 square feet, 0.00077 square yards	6.451 square centimetres

METRIC SYSTEM

Unit	Abbreviation		Approximate U.S. Equivalent		
		Length			
		Number of Metres			
myriametre	mym	10,000	6.2 miles		
kilometre	km	1000	0.62 mile		
hectometre	hm	100	109.36 yards		
dekametre	dam	10	32.81 feet		
metre	m	1	39.37 inches		
decimetre	dm	0.1	3.94 inches		
centimetre	cm	0.01	0.39 inch		
millimetre	mm	0.001	0.04 inch		
		Area			
		Number of Square Metres			
square kilometre	sq km *or* km²	1,000,000	0.3861 square miles		
hectare	ha	10,000	2.47 acres		
are	a	100	119.60 square yards		
centare	ca	1	10.76 square feet		
square centimetre	sq cm *or* cm²	0.0001	0.155 square inch		
		Volume			
		Number of Cubic Metres			
dekastere	das	10	13.10 cubic yards		
stere	s	1	1.31 cubic yards		
decistere	ds	0.10	3.53 cubic feet		
cubic centimetre	cu cm *or* cm³ *also* cc	0.000001	0.061 cubic inch		
		Capacity			
		Number of Litres	*Cubic*	*Dry*	*Liquid*
kilolitre	kl	1000	1.31 cubic yards		
hectolitre	hl	100	3.53 cubic feet	2.84 bushels	
dekalitre	dal	10	0.35 cubic foot	1.14 pecks	2.64 gallons
litre	l	1	61.02 cubic inches	0.908 quart	1.057 quarts
decilitre	dl	0.10	6.1 cubic inches	0.18 pint	0.21 pint
centilitre	cl	0.01	0.6 cubic inch		0.338 fluidounce
millilitre	ml	0.001	0.06 cubic inch		0.27 fluidram
		Mass and Weight			
		Number of Grams			
metric ton	MT *or* t	1,000,000	1.1 tons		
quintal	q	100,000	220.46 pounds		
kilogram	kg	1,000	2.2046 pounds		
hectogram	hg	100	3.527 ounces		
dekagram	dag	10	0.353 ounce		
gram	g *or* gm	1	0.035 ounce		
decigram	dg	0.10	1.543 grains		
centigram	cg	0.01	0.154 grain		
milligram	mg	0.001	0.015 grain		

Index

A

Abrasives. *See also* Sander belts; Sanders
  pumice powder, 29
  sanding discs, 28
  sandpaper, 24–28
  steel wool, 24, 28–29
  types of, 24
Accessories
  for router, 171, 172
  for table saw, 191
Accidents, visitors and, 21
Acrylic caulk, 44
Acrylic solvent
  applying to Plexiglas®, 132, 133
  description, 30
Adhesives. *See also* Epoxy glue; Glue; Rubber cement;
    Tape
  spray-on, 30, 31
  types, 29–31
Adhesive tape, removing, 194
African mahogany, 199
African rosewood, 199
Air-dried lumber, 97
American black walnut, 200–201
American cherry, 199
American elm, 199
Angle jigs, for radial arm saw, 152–153
Angles. *See also* Mitres
  accurate, with table saw, 192
  finding centers of, 31–32
  fine, with table saw, 192
  rafter, 170

Annual growth ring, 96
APA plywood
  performance standards for plywood, 143
  registered trademarks, 143
  sanded and touch-sanded, 146
  specialty panels, 145
Arbor hole, for circular-saw blade, reducing size of, 51
Arcs. *See* Circles
Auger bits, 64. *See also* Drill bits
Auxiliary base, for router, 171
Auxiliary table(s)
  for band saw, 36–37
  for drill press, 70–71
  for radial arm saw, 153
Avodire, 199
Awl, starting hole with, 32

B

Backsaw, 33
Band saw
  auxiliary tables for, 36–37
  circle cutting on, 37
  description, 34
  dowel cutting on, 38
  making duplicate cuts, 38
  making spiralled or fluted dowels with, 40–41
  rip fence, 38–40
  sanding with, 40
Band-saw blades
  cutting limitations of, 35

D

E

M

N

O

P

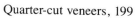

R

A Note from the Author

If you have any helpful woodworking shortcuts or jigs that you would like to share, send them, along with a rough sketch, to me, % Short Cuts, P.O. Box 721, Halifax, Nova Scotia, Canada B3N 2T3. I will test them in my workshop and, if they work, will try to find a place for them in future books. If I use them, I will give you credit.

Graham McCulloch